valuing
in the
family

A Workshop Guide for Parents

valuing
in the
family

A Workshop Guide for Parents

by

HERBERT O. BRAYER

Coordinator
Orange County Department of Education
Drug Abuse Prevention Education Center
Santa Ana, California

Formerly Associate State Superintendent of Public Instruction
State of Arizona

Formerly Coordinator
Innovative Solutions to Drug Abuse Prevention Education
Coronado Unified School District
Coronado, California

and

ZELLA W. CLEARY

Formerly Parent Workshop Associate
Innovative Solutions to Drug Abuse Prevention Education
Coronado Unified School District
Coronado, California

Published by

PENNANT PRESS

Library of Congress Catalog Card No. 72-93445
International Standard Book Number ISBN 0-913458-11-2

Seventh Printing February 1978

Printed in the United States of America

iv

Dedicated to

Kathy, Penny, Terry, Michael,
Cricket and Morgan

SO THEY MAY KNOW

Preface

Since the beginning of the teachers' workshops in the "valuing technique," and particularly since the beginning of the pilot project in the Coronado Unified School District, there has been a demand by many parents for a workshop in which they could learn the valuing techniques "so we can augment in the home what our children are learning in the classroom." This, supplemented by several discussions with Dr. Ray Rucker of United States International University, served as the initial stimulus for the development of a different parent approach to the behavioral problems of elementary and secondary students.

Another factor which led to our decision to attempt this workshop project was the realization that the traditional type "drug abuse-behavioral objectives" techniques which we had been using as part of the adult school program did not result in the goals we had hoped for . . . despite the fact that the parents involved almost unanimously felt that the program had been successful. In truth, we suspected the further we went along, the "standard" approach, that of developing a parent program strictly on a cognitive basis relating to the drug abuse problem, was not attaining the objectives we desired; which were primarily to help parents see that their actions (or lack of them) in the home and community environment strongly affect the behavioral patterns of their children, and that drug abuse was but one symptom of youth problems.

It was difficult in this strictly drug abuse program framework for parents to recognize the overall behavior pattern which results from both conscious and unconscious deprivations on the home and community fronts; for them to come to the place of acknowledging parental responsibility for a major portion of the deviant or anti-social behaviors originating in very young children, and which are reinforced with age as patterns become fixed through inflexible or provocative parental and community attitudes and behaviors.

It was with this sense of dissatisfaction that we determined to approach the parent education problem from an entirely different point of view — that of "valuing" as an approach to the behavior problem (which thereby included drug abuse as an important, though not necessarily central, factor). We hypothesized:

(1) If parents know and understand the process of valuing, they can augment what is being done in the school and thereby reinforce the enhancing process with their own children.

(2) Many student behaviors, it appeared, stemmed originally from family situations. Valuing would help parents to identify those positive as well as negative areas in which they contribute to their childrens' deprivations (with resulting behavioral problems), and those specific areas in which they can work positively on enhancing their childrens' needs and attitudes so as to avoid or alter such behavioral patterns. Lacking personal understanding of the process, its aims and techniques, parents could easily misunderstand the "valuing teaching process" and see it in the light of "permissiveness," or collectivistism and react accordingly. This type of parent workshop should provide a complete answer to this misunderstanding.

(3) Many "busy" parents state they "haven't time" to identify deprivation areas and to plan alternatives. Through open discussion the group environment should help them to see their own "hangups," as well as to help other parents in the group to identify and develop alternatives of their own to posed problem situations (i.e., identifying available coping behaviors or enhancing alternatives). In so doing the class would become "practical," and the terminology of the value categories would no longer be purely theoretical or academic, but become part of each adult participant's thinking as well as vocabulary.

(4) The valuing approach should help parents and their children to prevent or avoid a significant part of the alienation or "generation gap" which we found so prevalent among the hundreds of students with whom we worked in the program.

(5) If maximized, the valuing approach with parent groups should help to identify and find answers for the frequently expressed comment by teachers that "We and parents aren't going the same way at all." "Parents undo the good we do with their children, and don't understand our problems with their young ones." "There is a growing gap — credibility as well as respect — between us and parents."

(6) Taking the valuing techniques to parent groups should help create a common body of approaches to reach desired goals that will be understood and jointly developed by both parents and teachers, and could also be "translated" into community-wide involvement.

(7) The parent workshop should help get "feedback" from parents that can be used in designing new adult approaches for on-going workshops, parent conferences, adult education courses, and school-parent relationships.

(8) The parent workshop should help parents to see the major, as well as the minor, hypocrisies and inconsistencies that produce reaction and aberrant behavior among theirs and other children at all age levels regardless of ethnic or socio-economic backgrounds.

(9) Parents tend to perpetuate their own parents' attitudes and methods in raising their children, just as many teachers tend to perpetuate attitudes and methods learned early in their youth and teaching careers. This "ingraining" could be a major factor in causing youth problems, as well as causing parents to defend actions or attitudes they might not otherwise recognize were it not for the workshop method.

Herbert O. Brayer and Zella W. Cleary
Santa Ana, California
February, 1972

Contents

Introduction

During our family workshops, basic guidelines have emerged. Following them seems to assure a high level of success. Curiously enough, each one seems to work to the advantage of the group and aids in achieving the objectives of the workshop.

To avoid the "going to school" syndrome which many "young" adults seem to resent, parent-group sessions should not be held in schools or in any public institution. Both parents should attend the meetings because of their mutual involvement in "valuing in the family." (It is highly recommended that this mutual attendance be rigidly adhered to wherever possible.)

The participating parents should decide the meeting place, preferably one of their homes, for their ten week workshop. Sessions should be two hours long; the suggested time is 8 to 10 p.m. Because a "social hour" tends to create confusion and waste time, it should be established at the outset that there will be no smoking and no refreshments served before, during or after the sessions. The participants should realize that relaxation and congeniality should be within the discussion or workshop framework, rather than reserved for a food and drink period.

1

Experience has shown that each of the above recommendations contributes to the success of parent workshops. For example, in a typical workshop, not one person dropped from the course. There was a long waiting list of parents to take the next course. Participants arrived before the 8 p.m. scheduled starting time prepared to "get into the thick of things." No one, except in emergency situations, left the room and no attempts were made to offer cocktails or other refreshments. After the third meeting we were all on a first name basis, and, despite some intra-spouse bickering on a few occasions, there was an astounding amount of healthy repartee as well as congeniality during the otherwise serious discussions. This "hair down" frankness contributed to the learning atmosphere, and there seemed to be a ground swell building of "we don't want to quit this when the ten weeks are over."

Our approach took advantage of the flexibility of the group. Both of us shared in the presentation of the eight-category program and its delineation, but in doing so we completely avoided the familiar teacher-student-classroom approach and everything — including the category development — was concentrated on the parent-child-home relationship. A "how to" typescript of each category and its family "meaning" was prepared and distributed to each group member. Deliberately these were not reviewed in detail, but parents took them home, read them, and returned each week with specific examples of the successes and failures (problems) they may have had or were having in the specific categories under review. It was at this juncture that we found that the entire category "system" began to make sense and have distinct relevance to each person in the group and their approaches to their children.

There were disagreements, some very serious, between spouses on personal and family matters. It was clear that a no-holds barred relationship grew in the group with each passing week.   Our technique was to try to avoid the glib or quick answer and our "authority figures" as teachers. Each problem was thrown open to the group as soon as it was stated by a participant, and each member of the group was expected to express his or her opinion, and to offer possible alternatives or approaches. It was only after this usually highly-spirited "round robin" that one or both of us endeavored to sharpen up the points-at-issue and to summarize the concensus. On only a few points did we find ourselves differing with the participants' concensus, and these situations were discussed at length.

After the group had been meeting for three weeks they became familiar with almost all of the eight categories even though only three of the categories had been involved directly in the class "plan" up to that time. With this knowledge, the individual group members began to put together clusters of related categories (affection, well-being, rectitude; skill, enlightenment, wealth; respect, power, well-being).

We found considerable concern about the category of affection and its applicability to family as well as personal relationships between mother, father and siblings. The concept of respect bothered some parents of both sexes. The group spent considerable time evaluating the incident of a young boy who, having heard his mother say the family needed drinking glasses, went out and bought her a set of fancy stemware for a birthday or anniversary present. Instead of recognizing the affection and respect implicit in the gift, the mother berated the youngster for his inappropriate purchase, and further contributed to his chagrin and sense of deprivation by putting the glasses away and not using them. The boy (and his slightly older brother) continued to "bring up the glasses," and this still frustrated or irritated the parents.

Another instance also demonstrated the need for

emphasizing the importance of the affection and respect categories with children. One youngster purchased a somewhat garish wallet for his mother's Christmas present. She already had a good leather wallet that was in excellent condition. Again failing to recognize the importance of the matter to the youngster she "told him off" for having been so thoughtless, and took him back to the store where he had purchased the gift, and made him return it to the saleslady with an abject explanation. The effect on the youngster was recognized by the mother, but, despite his continued depression concerning it, she defended her action as teaching him responsibility. In both of the instances related, the group (individually and collectively) suggested alternatives that might have been taken which would have enhanced the child and still taught him skill at decision-making.

We found it necessary to keep repeating that what we were doing was trying to get at fundamental concepts, rather than to expect that every parent would be able to use all of the "tools" we included. Some parents – overwhelmed by a six or eight page roster of "do's" – couldn't see how they could put them all into effect. After discussing this at length, the group members realized that it was the overall picture that we were striving to enhance, and that no one or two parents could completely adopt such a comprehensive program on short notice. But that if they worked at it over a period of years, from birth on, almost every youngster would be affected) with his sense of well-being, his attitudes and his behavior positively developed.

"Do we always have to explain?" one parent asked. "Isn't there some time when we can just say 'no' without going into a discourse of 'why not'?" "Must we always refrain from corporal punishment to avoid the youngster feeling deprived?" "How far can or should we go when a child doesn't want to participate in family affairs, or to do his or her chores?" "What methods of punishment can be used that won't leave behavioral problems?" "Why don't my children owe respect to me?" "What can we do to make our son study when he just doesn't ever want to?" "Can't I ever just say 'do it because I say so,' or must I always go into a fifteen minute debate over the subject?" "How can I show my son that I really do love and want him when he is convinced that he is playing second-fiddle to his brother or sister?" "Gosh, I come home tired after eight, ten or twelve hours at work and I just want to collapse, not play fun and games with the kids; how do I get around this physical problem of mine that does affect my children?"

These are representative of the scores of questions and the long discussions our valuing workshops have dealt with. We've all learned a great deal: (1) accept the fact that no one has all the answers, and that there may not be readily available ones to all perplexing situations in a family; (2) recognize that each parent has his own limitations even when he knows what to do and can't do it; (3) trust, in most instances, the concensus of the group as being "common sense approaches," when the meaning of the category(ies) is truly trying to be implemented; (4) "don't bite off more than you can chew," (for example, we've never yet been able to fully complete a lesson plan laid out for a session! The workshop technique will more often than not force you to jettison a pre-planned outline! Accept this and use the "happenings" that arise as the working areas for that particular meeting.) (5) Watch out for intra-family disagreements — don't get trapped into taking sides or being used by one partner against another. (6) An effort should be made to keep the verbage simple and direct, and to keep the group from getting onto pure theory or philosophy if it can possibly be avoided.

Affection

AFFECTION
Definition: To establish and maintain in the home a deep sense of emotional security, love, caring, congeniality, interest and friendship in all phases of both individual and group life.

Affection refers to the degree of love, caring, and friendship of persons in their primary as well as secondary relationships — those within the family or group and those outside of the immediate family or group. Necessarily this must include love for and loyalty toward groups, organizations, one's city, state and nation. For the child or adult whose behavior is conditioned by dislike, fear and/or hatred of other human beings, the future can hold but little promise for development of a mature personality or a stable relationship with others.

One of the primary goals of the family, therefore, must be to identify and supplant as early in life as possible fears and hatreds which embitter the individual and lead to extreme personality damage. Affection, regard and genuine concern for others, is a motivating value goal which parents must not only have for themselves but assist their children to attain.

It is unfortunate that such a large number of children at all ages somehow come to feel unloved, unwanted and unimportant — even to themselves. To offset or prevent the formation of such attitudes parents must work deliberately with each child starting as early as possible to develop a widespread sharing of affection in the home. It is in this sharing that human relationships mature and contribute to consistent progress toward democracy.

A. Parents — equally both mother and father — must make concerted daily efforts to establish and maintain congenial, understanding relationships with each child in the family.

   1. Each parent strives to treat each child *consistently* in an affectionate manner.

      a. Father and mother strive to greet each child cheerfully each morning. ("The breakfast attitude is likely to become the days attitude.")

      b. Father as well as mother seek genuine cheer and humor in recognizing each child throughout the day.

      c. Both parents use any favorable moment to spark a conversation with their children — before school, after school and in the evening.

      d. When possible, parents take all meals with their children. The family "table" is an ideal place for family conferences, discussions, information gathering, planning, and decision-making, but *not* for argument or contention.

      e. Parents should try to attain a high degree of consistency in dealing with each child. Playing with the child one moment and ignoring him the next confuses the child, and leads him to doubt your sincerity or the depth of your affection.

f. Parents should practice and try to develop a calm, affectionate, and understanding manner when the child errs, fails to follow through on a chore, or requests help at an inopportune moment.

g. Father as well as mother should help and participate in family humor, jokes, story telling and even harmless tricks — even though father or mother are the objects of such humor.

h. Sharing the TV set or radio along with sharing the chores (and they should have responsibilities at even the tender ages) help build a sense of belonging that equates with affection. Asking children for their opinions and ideas — and listening to them with appropriate responses — help the child to build his sense of security and love of parents and family.

i. Sharing the amenities at bedtime — making a game of it with the youngest and a moment of sincerity with the older ones reveals the depths of affection that build family solidarity and individual security.

2. Each parent strives to take an individual interest in each child each day.

a. Father and mother find those precious moments — if possible each day — for a private word with each child; for an informal expression of interest or concern; for a short discussion or play at the child's interest or hobby.

b. Sometime during the week each parent seeks (if the opportunity doesn't automatically present itself) a "heart to heart," "man to man," or "girl talk" session with each child. These should be strictly "private" affairs for each parent and child — a time to unload, to discuss worrisome problems or fears.

c. Father when reading the paper seeks deliberately some point, squib or comic that he can casually bring up with the children (individually, if possible). This not only builds the affection link but helps heighten interest in what is going on.

d. Both parents (separately if desirable, but together is preferable) discuss each child's school achievement record (report cards) unless it would be embarrassing for the child to have this done in front of other children, in which case it can be done in the "heart to heart" sessions. The child must know that you are not just interested in his grades, but in his true achievements as well as his school problems. Don't say, "Well, I love you even if you are a dope," when you can use the situation to build a positive rather than negative relationship — and do so without implying *acceptance* of low achievement or failure. Put this, too, into perspective — let the child know of your concern FOR HIM, not your pique because his record hurts your sense of pride or prestige!

e. If at all possible play daily outside with your children even if it is at dusk. Find sometime in which you (both father and mother) join with your children in *their activities* rather than always seeking to have them join in yours.

f. Take notice of achievement and actions of each child individually and make sure you comment positively to each. Preserve the feeling of individual concern even when developing the family or group effort.

g. Plan well in advance — so as to avoid conflicts in engagements — to attend your children's school affairs (plays, recitals, back-to-school events, etc.) Your child will carefully note when other mothers and fathers show up for class or school events and you do not. He'll try to understand when you can't make it, but if it is repeated he'll acquire the oft-heard attitude, "they really don't care about me." Surveys show this is becoming a serious personality attitude with deprivation results.

h. Physical contact is an important part of the Affection category to children. An arm around his waist or a pat on the head, a squeeze of the hand, etc., all have a meaningful relations to the child (young and old) and to his Affection ratio. Non-verbal communication in this category is very important and should not be overlooked as part of the healthy expression of both individual as well as family appreciation and cohesiveness.

i. Encourage relationships between your children and other family members — aunts, uncles, grandparents, godparents, etc. Affection can be healthily reinforced by broad-

ening the child's realization of the depth
with which he is regarded by many family
members, relatives and friends.

j. Give special care to the shy or affection-
    starved child (but guard against other
    brothers and sisters getting the idea of
    favoritism). Develop an acuteness of your
    child's feelings and interpret those that
    reflect unusual tensions. At times a child will
    be troubled but will not communicate his
    "problem" or seek help. You will have to
    take the initiative in such instances and
    should do so promptly. (Try not to allow a
    child to go to bed feeling deprived!)

k. Teasing can be an important aid in over-
    coming affection deprivation when lightly
    and humorously used.

B. When hostilities arise, prompt and deliberate efforts
   should be taken by parents to restore friendly
   attitudes.

   1. Each parent tries to overcome family hostilities
      by his or her attitude and actions.

      a. Parents do not place their children in a
          position where they will openly have to
          oppose each other or compete unfairly.

      b. Parents recognize hostilities which arise and
          do not try to suppress them by ignoring
          them, but rather seek to deal realistically
          with them. If the problem cannot be mutual-
          ly resolved with both or all children involved
          in a dispute, you may have to resort to
          private conferences with an upset youngster.
          Assist and encourage him to tell his side of
          the story, thus relieving some of the tension,

but refrain from taking sides until all have been heard.

c. Make light of embarrassing situations and joke about them to relieve tensions (but avoid making the child the butt of the joke).

d. Separate children involved in hostile attitudes or acts until you can handle each separately and work for reproachment. Do not force a change; attitudes are not successfully altered by force! If possible, put "feuding" children together in situations where there is no inherent tension, and where it will be easy for friendly relations to be resumed without residual feelings from the difficulty.

2. Children try to overcome hostilities with and among their sisters, brothers and peers.

a. By developing cheerful, confident attitudes towards all competing brothers, sisters and friends, children tend to discourage their hostile actions.

b. Children talk to each participant in an effort to get him to consider the unreality of his aggressive behavior.

c. Both boys and girls actually separate other siblings and peers who are about to get into an action which might cause them to harm each other.

d. Following disagreements, children offer each other opportunities to get together under favorable circumstances (or parents should provide the opportunity and let their children take advantage of it).

    e. Children must make an attempt (with parent help at the outset) *to understand the causes* of some of the hostile acts of their brothers, sisters and peers, and often allow them to get tensions out of their systems by encouraging them to express feelings orally without taking offense.

    f. Children show respect for brothers, sisters and peers who actively try to avoid conflicts with others.

    g. Children's attitudes are definitely favorable to those who do not hold grudges, but who attempt to be friends again after an argument.

C. Definite efforts should be made to reduce adverse and unnecessary criticism of family members and friends.

    1. Criticism of individuals must be constructive.

        a. Encourage children not to criticize just by saying that something is wrong. Strive to get them to give reasons why they disagree with it.

        b. When advice is requested children should offer suggestions on how a brother or sister can perform more effectively.

        c. Youthful family members should not make it a practice to offer criticism unless it is requested.

        d. Negative criticism is not offered (even when asked) unless there is a positive suggestion as to how the condition or situation could be improved.

        e. Parents and older brothers and sisters should

strictly avoid serious criticism of other family members when anyone else is present.

f.   Fathers and mothers must develop timely occasions where all children are given an opportunity to make remarks about the other's performances so that all will get accustomed to accepting suggestions without tension and resentment.

2.   Group criticism is always made in an effort to improve the product of the group.

   a.   Group criticism is offered in a helpful spirit; avoid personality conflicts.

   b.   Criticism of individuals and groups should avoid prejudicial and emotional comments relative to race, color or creed or socially embarrassing circumstances and situations.

   c.   All constructive criticism should be offered and received in a cheerful and cooperative manner, and in a positive vein.

   d.   Parents should work together and with their children to develop an approach that seeks to find good points about each family member, and to give recognition to these rather than to any difficult mannerisms.

   e.   Disapproval of undemocratic or thoughtless practices by children is frequently and successfully shown by the absence of a smile and approval. A parent can simply praise the child who is acting in ways opposite to the offender, thus pointing up the offense, i.e., "Johnny, I do like the way you stand when mother comes to the table — so tall and straight and ready to help her with her chair."

D. Any denial of affection is directed only against the conduct which is incompatible with democratic goals in the family, not the person.

1. Overt denial of affection by father or mother is practiced only in serious cases of anti-social conduct and then only on a temporary basis.

   a. Children who do not play fair at home are asked to play alone for awhile.

   b. Children who continually or unnecessarily disturb other family members at dinner, during study, when company is present, or at otherwise inconvenient times are asked to sit by themselves or to leave the room.

   c. Children who consistently fail to follow the rules or to do their assigned tasks at home may not be included *in some* of the family projects in which they enjoy taking part, and are given straightforward reasons why these actions have been taken. (Parents do NOT perform the unfinished tasks *or get other children in the family to do so,* even if the situation is temporarily inconvenient. The child must learn responsibility but should not be deprived of affection while being temporarily penalized. All penalties should fit the offense and the child must understand that a penalty is assessed for that specific reason, and does not affect his security and affection within the family group.)

2. Parents and other children in the family restore the status of a child who has committed an anti-social act when that member again practices conduct which recognizes his responsibility and the rights of other family members.

    a. Efforts are made to bring children who consistently rebel into a more congenial relationship with other family members.

       (1) Mother and Father — or other brothers and sisters — encourage the "rebel" to join with them in family activities; particularly pleasant tasks or opportunities.

       (2) A search is made to identify special talents of rebellious family members and to recognize and encourage these.

       (3) No "publicity" or big show is attached to the "returning to the fold" of a child who has been involved in an anti-social scene or behavior.

E. Parents should remember alternatives which will enhance the affection category and reinforce their childrens' understanding.

   1. A pat on the back for a good piece of work at home or at school; a word of comfort to the child who may have been emotionally or physically hurt may mean more than anything else because he believes that someone really cares about him.

   2. Even four to six-year olds have problems which are too big for them. If mother and father will only take *time to listen* and offer serious and thoughtful suggestions, it will lighten their burdens.

   3. Parents should encourage the development of secondary affection relationships — such as learning and knowing what the pledge to the flag really means and the singing of the national, state and school anthems.

4. Parents must help their children to know other children in the neighborhood. Making friendships is important. Parents can and should get together with other parents to develop social opportunities (and to provide security). Parties, picnics, games, etc., are natural and desirable methods of developing socially acceptable behavioral patterns and attitudes in a democratic society.

5. Parents should encourage even the youngest of their children to develop high activity quotients — to take part with other children and family members in a broad range of activities. While every child should have time to be with himself in quiet play and rest, this must not be allowed to develop into an unhealthy condition (and that goes for permitting him to sit hour after hour before the "boob-tube").

6. Remember to recognize each child's right to privacy and to his own opinions, but be ever present to help with challenging personal problems when he wants and needs you.

Some Ideas and Worksheets for Improving Affection

Remember to always keep "natural." Don't try to do everything at once or all the time. Variety is the "spice of life" but *consistency* in the application of the Affection concept from birth to maturity (and indeed throughout adult life as well) is the key to enhancement of the universal "need and want." It is that consistency, sincere and not forced, that pays off!

Study the following suggestions and try them as the occasion and interest arises.*

Workshop assignments will be made at meetings if any of these are to be part of the group activity.

DISCUSSIONS AND ACTIVITIES
WITH YOUR CHILDREN

Instructions: NOT to be done all at once but gradually and as opportunities occur.

1. **DISCUSS:**

    a. Who do you like and why? Make a list in order of your "likes."

    b. Who do you dislike and why? Make a list in order of your "dislikes."

    c. Analyze the "why's" — are they because you are jealous or afraid of the person?

    d. What is the difference between:

    Loving
    Caring
    Friendship
    Loyalty

2. How did you greet your children this morning (each one)? How did they react or respond? (If you try consistently every day for one week see if you can notice a difference the seventh morning.)

3. What game or activity do you play or do with your children (individually or collectively) this week?

4. Did you *find* time for private conversations with each child?

5. Worksheet: (a) Family Activities this week (list)? (b) What tentative family activities have you planned for this week?

6. Take one day and make an honest effort to count the number of times you were negative or reacted negatively. Take the next day and see if you can be positive all day and tabulate your successes and failures (if any).

7. Have a Criticism "Board" — anytime one member of the family makes a serious criticism of another it is written on a black or chalk board. Later, after it has been read, it is discussed and an effort made to judge whether it is true or false and the person involved has a right to respond. Each criticism is ended when suggestions are made for overcoming the fault.

CONSTRUCTIVE CRITICISM

How can you change the following into enhancement statements, rather than the feisty, deprivational ones they are now that set up instantaneous resentment and rebellious attitudes?

1. "Your hair is awful and makes you look like a bum! Go get it cut or get out!"

2. "Your room is a filthy mess. Clean it up or I'll whale the daylights out of you."

3. "When are you going to learn to do something right?"

4. "I've never seen such writing; now sit down and write a 'Thank You Letter' that Grandma can read."

5. "You talk too loud. Your dress is too loud. You're always acting out. You always criticize your mother and father. You're never satisfied and you make our lives miserable, too."

6. "You're lazy and worthless. I don't know how you'll ever amount to anything!"

7. "When are you going to learn how to get people to like you? No wonder boys don't ask you to parties and dances!"

8. "If you don't study your lessons, you'll end up on welfare, or just be a failure the rest of your life."

9. "I advise you to mend you ways, young man, or you'll end up in Juvenile Hall, even if I have to put you there myself."

10. "If you don't stop picking on your brother I'll start picking on you, and you'll really be sorry."

WORK SHEET

Make a column for each of your children and indicate after their names or initials their ages. Under each name list (a) the responsibilities you have given each one. After each entry put a (d) for daily; (w) for weekly; (bm) bi-monthly; (m) monthly, to indicate how often the child is expected to complete all or part of the responsibility.

Example:

Jane (3)

1. Pick up toys. (d)

2. Hang up clothes. (d)

3. Carry clothes in from laundry room and put away. (w)

Billy (8)

1. Straighten out room. (d)

2. Take out garbage. (bw)

3. Clean up cat or dog refuse in yard. (d or w)

4. Help mow lawn and dig weeds. (w)

5. Say "Grace" for family at meals. (rotation)

ACTIVITY WORK SHEET
(Make One for Father and One for Mother)

Again in each column put the initials of each of your children. Set up a calendar for the next two weeks and in each column list the *specific personal activities* you engage in with each child (i.e. party, picnic, theater, zoo, "visit to Grandma's," bowling, church, school conference, musical or music lesson, shopping, private talk or "listening" session, sports — playing with or taking them with you to a game, playing Monopoly or other indoor games, etc., etc.). Be sure to list *only* those child-oriented activities designed or intended to specifically enhance the child (in other words, do not include activities which are solely for your convenience or benefit, but, *do* include activities which are for helping your child to learn and complete tasks.

Example:

Jane (3)

Mon. 1st: Took shopping.
Played "Cootie."
Tues. 2nd: Helped me with knitting yarn.
Blew soap bubbles together.

Wed. 3rd: Dressed & took her to Sally's birthday party and helped serve.

Frank (9)

1st: Shopping for shirts and bathrobe — he selected.
2nd: Helped him repair hole in basketball.
Served him and friends cookies & chocolate after basketball.

Helped him with his math.
3rd: Helped with "Star-Chart" for trip to observatory.

Billy (8)

1st: Shopping for school shoes & trousers with me — let him choose them.
Helped correct spelling.
Helped with Cub Scout requirements.
2nd: Tossed ball with him.
Help finish new arrows.

Took him to Jimmy's for Little League meeting.
3rd: Showed him how to put iron-on patches on torn blue jeans.
Played Monopoly with him after hearing him read.

Etc., Etc.

PROBLEM WORK SHEET

1. *Name (initials) of child:*   *Age:*

2. Define the problem as you see it (not more than 25 words but get to the heart of it):

3. Define the problem as the child sees it *(in his or her words, not yours)*:

4. At what points do you differ in defining the problem?

   a. your point: his/her point:

   b. your point: his/her point:

   c. your point: his/her point:

5. What specific *areas for compromising* (mutually agreeing) are there on each of the points in No. 4?

6. In *his/her words* what *areas for compromising* are there on each point?

7. List three *alternatives* that you think would solve the problem from your point of view.

   a.

   b.

   c.

8. List three *alternatives* that he/she thinks would best solve the problem from his/her point of view.

    a.

    b.

    c.

9. Both of you examine the other's *alternatives* and determine in order which you could accept (even with *some* alterations to meet each ones ideas):

10. Decide which alternative you will accept (or *which will come closest* to resolving the problem from both points of view). Agree on it and consider the problem solved until or unless it arises again. If it does, repeat the process altering or eliminating the *alternatives* that failed to solve the problem the first time.

"LISTENING" WORK SHEET

After a child has discussed a situation (at home or at school, etc.) take a few moments to analyze what the child said and how you responded. The following list may help you to come to grips with the listening problem (many children tell teachers, friends, and relatives openly that "my father — or mother — never listens to me." "They don't really hear what I'm saying." "They won't take time to let me tell it my way, or the way I see it." "They really don't care about my side, they only know what they want." etc., etc.)

1. Shorn of excess verbiage, just what did the child say (repeat exact words if you can; the *choice of words* may be important)?

2. Who were the others involved in the incident, story, request or explanation?

   a. Names and ages.

   b. What do you *really* know about each of the others? (Watch your prejudices or biases.)

   c. What role (participation) did or will each play in the story or incident?

   d. Evaluate the role each played in the light of what your child said and what you know or find out.

3. Why did your child relate the incident, story, request or explanation?

    a. Excuse? (If so, why did he/she feel it necessary?)

    b. Was the child "fishing" for support, relief, assistance, approval or help?

4. Was your child trying to tell you something about herself/himself or others without really saying what was on her/his mind? List possibilities? (Example: Mary went into a long discussion about what certain of her friends "told her" about their trying marijuana — or taking "pills" — and the "fun" they had. While she put on an air of disapproval, her voice had an interested or excited tone. Was she really saying she was curious and would like to try it and find out for herself? Was she obliquely telling you she had tried it and disapproves — or indeed did find it "fun" and wanted to draw out your opinion?)

5. What kind of answer did you give? Did you consider the matter logically and impersonally? Did you fly off the handle and preach or threaten? Did you indicate understanding and suggest how he/she could find for themselves the answers, alternatives, or other views? Did you come over as loving and understanding parent or an up-tight purist, theoretical, unknowledgeable, or "hard-line" Establishment figure?

6. Did the child go away feeling satisfied and understood, or "put down," deprived, "put off," or threatened?

FAMILY HISTORY WORKSHOP
To enhance Loyalty, Belonging
(not alienated or lost)

Make a family project out of preparing a real geneology (both sides of the family if possible) which has the objective of showing youngsters they really are a part of something that is wholly theirs. Make it interesting not only by names and dates of birth, baptisms, marriages, deaths, but by making real people out of ancestors in such a way that the child can connect himself directly with the past.

Example: John F. Smith (great, great, great paternal grand-father) born, 1743 in Boston, Mass., died 1831 in Zanesville, Ohio, married Rebecca J. Wright, daughter of *French and Indian War* veteran under *George Rogers Clark,* co-founder of Zanesville, Ohio, farmer, and friend of *Wapunka,* famed Indian Chief. John Smith fought in *Washington's* army and helped win the *American Revolution* and *freedom.* He had a *grammar school education but left school* to go West with his father. Obtained land in Ohio with *veterans benefits* (land script); cleared land of forest and farmed; opened a leather (saddlery) shop in Zanesville. Was going *to go to Texas* but became ill of *cholera* and died as there was *no cure* for the disease at that time.

Italicized words are those with which your child can relate as he hears or studies about them in school, at home, and on TV. He begins to see himself as directly related not just to his family but to important people and events. The more he relates the deeper he feels "his roots (belonging) go." The more this is done the more successful its potential good for the child. Parents can reverse the order and start with father (who went to Vietnam or was Mayor, etc.), or Uncle Mort who left his job and served in Korea or World War II; or in Africa as a Peace Corpsman, or as a judge, writer, scientist, miner, railroad builder, machinist or earth machine operator. The key is to have the child play an active role in assembling or writing up the materials, in finding and mounting pictures, etc. Involve the children at every point and do the job consistently − once a week regularly or twice a month. Explain how we can trace and get records made hundreds of years ago.

Secondary purpose is to get the child to recognize that he has the same family background and the same or better opportunities to be successful in what he wants to do. It's not who or what his ancestors were but who and what he is, using the talents and abilities and motivations he has, that will decide whether he, too, will someday be a part of someone's proud heritage.

References and Guides for your help in working with your children on geneologies:

1.

2.

3.

4.

5.

Respect

Definition: Providing an atmosphere in which your child may employ his individual talents with success in achieving a recognized social role and self-esteem without fear of undeserved deprivation or penalties from parents, peers, or others, and in which he, in turn, can find adult and peer models to whom he can give respect and honor.

"One of the most important needs of the human being is that he be respected by his fellowman . . . one of the most important contributions to man's mental health is the knowledge that he is accorded recognition based upon the merit of his accomplishments . . . THIS APPLIES TO THE CHILD . . . AT ALL AGE AND GRADE LEVELS AS WELL AS TO THE ADULT THROUGHOUT HIS LIFE" (W.R. Rucker *Human Values in Education*).

Points to consider:

1. The significance for the child in securing *respect for himself.* It is the index of his confidence.

2. In order to have respect for you and other members of his family, teachers, and others he must FIRST have respect for himself. Like all other value categories, respect must be shared.

3. If parents show no respect for each other – or for themselves personally – the child will find it very difficult to develop respect for them. (Don't confuse "love" with "respect.") Parents who lack respect for themselves and each other cannot be expected to be successful in promoting respect among their children.

4. Parents with a moderate to high sense of respect tend to face their problems realistically with a minimum of substitution, self-deception and retreat.

5. Consequences of respect deprivation are most serious in terms of personality damage. (Can result in hostility, guilt transference, way out behavior, delinquency, mental illness, etc.)

A. Respect is accorded every member of the family *on the basis of merit.*

   1. Each child should have the opportunity to explain problems he faces in his daily life at home, school and at play. (Parents should see that the opportunity is regular and that they truly listen and discuss each situation.) Respect your child's privacy.

   2. Clarify uncertainty and lack of understanding.

   3. Teach and allow child to practice self-discipline whenever possible.

   4. Make certain each child has daily opportunity to participate in family life.

   5. Not only should each parent show courtesy and respect to children ("Thank You" and "Please," etc.), but insist upon courteous behavior to all brothers and sisters as well as parents. "Thank You" and "Please" and other widely accepted amenities are highly effective in according re-

spect, but you should teach sincerity in their use.

6. Don't employ sarcasm as an instrument of management. It is resented, internalized, and copied. It does NOT work successfully over a period of time regardless of its immediate effect.

7. Regardless of the provocation, speak to your children in a calm, dignified and courteous way and DO NOT SHOUT AT THEM. You are the model they will copy. Remember that many children are mirror-images of their parents. The most effective parent approach is not to permit yourself to become irate, and to approach each problem with deliberate calmness.

8. Not only should parents respect a child's property rights, but they should teach and insist each child (from 1 year of age onwards) respect each other's property rights. (This does not mean to encourage selfishness. Encourage sharing together, but let it be plain that every person in the family is entitled to what is his.)

9. Encourage each child to take part in family discussions, and make sure you do have such discussions (about vacations, shows, picnics, church, school, holidays, visits, problems, etc., etc.)

10. Assume your child is telling the truth until proved otherwise. (This may be difficult at times, but exaggeration and fantasy are part of every normal child's world so care must be used not to deprive the child of respect by calling him a liar or in inferring his lack of credibility.) (Here the axiom must be for the dubious parent, "It's not what you do as much as the way you do it.")

11. Permit each child to participate in family affairs *so long as his behavior merits it.* (Make sure the offender understands that he deprived himself of participation by his actions; that it was not you that did it. This assumes that the "rules" have been made perfectly clear and understandable on several recent occasions.)

12. Family members who have special talents should be recognized for their use of such talents — publicly patted on the back and recognized as well as encouraged. (But make sure you find some way to recognize EACH child, not just the obviously talented one.) Encourage the talented one to help others to achieve their own success in their own way.

13. From the beginning of a child's family life insist that he listen intently to what his brothers and sisters are saying.

14. Use corporal punishment (striking or shaking) with great care and then in private, if at all possible. Punishment must be just, prompt and should be done in calmness if it is to have its greatest positive effect. When done in anger or anxiety it frequently produces just the opposite effect to that which the parent wanted.

    To be spanked or reprimanded in public inflicts double punishment — the direct one you inflict and that which results from having one's peers or others see the humiliation. Tests show clearly that this one area has created more deviant and serious behavior than almost any other factor except lack of affection and well-being.

15. Notice and warmly comment when a child shows courtesy and respect to others.

16. Recognize publicly every achievement or honor your child attains. This builds his confidence, respect for himself as well as for whatever the activity he was engaged in, and sets an example for other children. Of great importance is the fact that it builds motivation for children.

17. Select children to perform errands, activities or chores based on something more than age and straight assignment of tasks. Make them a sign of your respect for them — recognizing their abilities, sense of responsibility, maturing, role in life ("growing up"), etc.

18. Encourage your child to take the personal "risk" of participating in something he has not previously tried. Illustrate that "failure" is not disgrace, that all people fail to a degree; that the only real failure is when one doesn't try — and try again.

B. Discrimination requires parental attention to every phase of their children's daily lives both in the family and outside.

1. Every child merits respect because he is a human being. It makes no difference whether the child is gifted, talented, retarded, mischievious or angelic; he or she should learn that because he is human he should expect to receive *and to give* respect.

2. Do not discriminate among your children because of conditions beyond their control.

   a. Each child differs in talents, skills and ability as well as intelligence. Avoid comparisons and recognize each child for himself. (Respect and self-esteem are not generated when a child feels himself less appreciated, less recognized, "put down," compared unfavorably with a younger or older sibling. The result almost invariably is personality damage.)

b. Avoid "favorites." Children recognize parental actions, and react in serious ways to obvious favoritism among peers. Guard against the "hand-me-down" complex even though such may be effectively used and needed.

3. Teach your child effectively *not* to discriminate because of race, color or creed, or socio-economic backgrounds of his peers.

a. Prejudice is a "learned" characteristic; children are not born with it. Avoid the hate words and expressions that promote racial discrimination.

b. Encourage each child to learn about other people and to challenge false generalizations. Have them study how other peoples live and play, eat and work. Use customs, music, colorful costumes (dolls), food, etc., which are easily seen and deserve respect based on their merit. Emphasize similarities of needs and wants (universal "values") rather than obvious differences.

c. Encourage children to choose friends from various backgrounds because of personal compatibility, values, standards, mutual interests rather than race, color or creed. Teach them to give respect on the basis of personal merit. (Individualism.)

C. Give positive help in overcoming handicaps that might otherwise prevent your child from achieving the respect status he needs and wants.

1. Work patiently with your child so that he acquires the skill to perform tasks successfully, and can build *his* self-esteem and secure respect from others.

2. Discover what your child likes to do, and then teach and provide him with the opportunity to do it well. (Every child must have something he knows he excels in.)

3. Make sure each child has an opportunity to display (to father, family and friends) examples of his best efforts.

4. Refer personality problems that demand professional attention to recognized and state licensed therapists, psychologists and psychiatrists. Do it promptly and don't second guess these experts.

5. Aid your child to accept handicaps and help him constantly to overcome their ill-effects. Don't make reference to these handicaps in front of the child in such a way that they will "hurt" or make him feel less capable or competent.

6. Encourage each child to take part positively in group activities as well as individual ones. Illustrate how he can make a contribution to group success or accomplishments. Handicapped children who can't take part in group activities should be encouraged to do things that others will see, hear, take part in, etc., such as writing stories or playlets, drawing pictures of group activities, keeping score, officiating, etc.

7. Recognize *warmly* unusual helpfulness or co-operation, thus encouraging the development of personality traits which help develop respect both within and outside of the family.

8. With mentally handicapped children, parents need patience and dedication in helping to develop traits and skills which will enable the child to gain respect for himself as well as from others. This should not be confused with being permissive.

   a. With professional guidance set up a definite plan for assistance.

   b. Try to avoid emotional situations which the child cannot handle.

   c. Teach the child to understand his handicap and how to cope with it.

   d. Recognize and compliment the child on each sign of progress he makes, and encourage other family members to do the same. Keep emphasizing the need for patience on the part of all members of the household.

D. Sharing is one of the principal keys to attaining and holding respect.

   1. Concentrate on sharing activities, participation with others.

   2. Concentrate on getting children to "listen," not just to you but to each other.

   3. Teach youngsters to answer the door, telephone, and to assume their share of responsibility for a smoothly operating family by making it a "fun" as well as a respect-achieving accomplishment.

   4. Provide opportunities — if they fail to show up normally — for recognition of each child's good points.

   5. Allow children to help (even though it may make more work for you in the end).

6. Ask the child's opinion on anything that he feels is important, and anything you feel would enhance his feeling of self respect.

7. Listening to children, really listening, is a very effective technique of according them respect. Keep open all channels of parent-child communication regardless of stress and strain.

8. Be courteous even in disciplinary situations. It is more effective if you calmly but firmly say, "Sit down *please!*" rather than shout "SIT DOWN!" Courtesy is a "key" to respect!

9. Encourage each child to exploit his strong points.

10. Share your beliefs with your children, but show respect for theirs (they'll probably change their beliefs so often, anyway, that to do otherwise would only make issues when it is counter productive).

11. Encourage each child to help the others.

12. Avoid laughing AT or ridiculing your child regardless of provocation. You both lose in such cases!

SUGGESTIONS FOR ATTAINING AND MAINTAINING RESPECT IN THE FAMILY

Here again, the following are purely suggestive and potentially satisfying ways any family can use to promote the universal need for "respect." They are also designed to promote the "sharing" of respect since value can only be really enjoyed when a person gives respect as well as seeks and receives it.

Again the key is consistency. If you are respectful only part of the time the child becomes confused and is likely to wonder just which personality is really yours. Sincerity must be a part of respect otherwise the child will see you as having ulterior purposes and hypocritical.

Study the suggestions and try them as the opportunity arises.

WORKSHEET

1. Name five people for whom you have respect? Why?

person		reason
a.	=	
b.	=	
c.	=	
d.	=	
e.	=	

2. Name five reasons why you want people to respect you:

   a.

   b.

   c.

   d.

   e.

3. Give five specific *factual (not emotional)* reasons why you respect this country and briefly explain each in simple terms:

   a.

b.

c.

d.

e.

4. Why do people, even his oldest and most intimate friends, call the President of the United States "Mr. President," instead of using his first name as they always did before he was elected President?

5. Why do we say or write:

    a. Dr. Jones instead of Mr. Jones?

    b. Reverend Smith instead of Mr. Smith?

    c. Professor Mack instead of Mr. Mack?

    d. Honorable John Doakes instead of John Doakes?

    e. His Eminance Bishop Frank Daughtery instead of Mr. Daughtery?

6. Can you add four other titles that we use to show respect for people or positions they hold?

    a.

    b.

    c.

    d.

    e.

WORKSHOP

1. Explain – Why do we keep yards clean and neat?

2. Explain – Why do we refrain from swearing or telling off-color stories?

3. Explain – Why do we dress "up" to go to church and to a dedication or installation?

4. Explain – Why do we help invalids, the elderly or others to do heavy tasks or jobs?

5. Explain – Why do we stand up (and uncover our heads) when the flag is marched by or the national anthem played?

Look at the *First Ten Amendments to the Constitution* and explain how each specifically refers to "respect" for each individual, regardless of race, color, creed, wealth or position in society. Show how each also refers to home and family affairs.

SHARING

List 10 *important* ways in which we (parents with children, children with children) do or can share daily at home:

1.

2.

3.

4.

5.

6.

7.

8.

9.

10.

What do the following words in the *Pledge of Allegiance* actually mean? (Each has a specific "Respect" connotation.)

1. "And to the Republic . . ."

2. "One nation indivisible"

3. "Liberty"

4. "Justice for all"

5. "Under God"

Explain: "No one, except by force, can demand respect."

"Respect, even by one's children, is *earned daily* rather than assumed as a right.

Enlightenment

Definition: To provide opportunities for each child to learn, to inquire and to discover truth in every situation, circumstance and issue while gaining understanding of social norms and the significant events of history.

Here the objective is to make sure that you as a parent help children to learn from what they see, hear, and do at home and in the community. Every experience is a learning one *provided* that while children are young you help them to see and understand what they have learned. Encourage *active participation* followed by explanation of what was learned and understanding of its application. Children do learn "automatically" but frequently it is superficial if parents don't *help* the youngster to see the full learning possibilities.

You can pinpoint opportunities to make a learning situation out of the ordinary events of the day — from getting up, dressing, eating breakfast, etc.

A. Use family communications (discussions, books, magazines, encyclopedias, films, photographs, radio, television, etc.)

B. Father and mother serve as observers, teachers and guides.

   1. Parents continue their own education (formal or informal — reading, social events, arts, sciences, music, etc.)
   2. Parents analyze and appraise their own experiences at work, in the community and in the family.
   3. Guide children and arouse interest in family backgrounds, cultures, arts, science, and music and make a point of answering childrens' questions (*not necessarily all questions*). Seek to guide children to find their own answers and arrive at their own values and decisions while broadening their interests to the *maximum.*

C. Discussion with children regularly — reasonable effort to establish authenticity and truth. Again stimulate the child to do his own inquiry then listen to him and if he is willing help him check the results.

D. Establish respect for knowledge and scholarship at all family levels — compliment and recognize achievement for home learning as well as school. Encourage school achievement but don't make it a fetish. (Environment helps condition "Enlightenment" — the presence and use of books, magazines, dictionaries, newspapers, reports, radio and TV, visits, travel, etc.)

E. Encourage each child to recognize his or her own abilities and capabilities (including limitations he must learn to live with), and set *own* standards of achievement.
   1. Allow children to make their own choices or decisions based on their desired goals, but discuss the basis for them, if possible before decisions are made (live with the decision made

by your child *if at all possible*).

2. Remember that the key to enlightenment is activity. Encourage children to participate — scouting, camping, church activities, helping you — and recognize their effort and success, minimal though it may be.

3. Children should be given assistance to set up standards concerning their hobbies and interests and encouraged to do worthwhile work in these areas. This could include community enterprises in hospitals, nurseries, churches, and other organizations where a child learns by working with others.

F. At all levels of maturity, and daily, encourage each child to make an analysis of the important events in which he takes part — why should he get up on time; why should he eat breakfast; why should he keep clean; why should he go to school; why should he learn art and music; what programs on television should he select; and what programs should he not select by his own choice.

Get the child to verbalize his reasons. Start slowly but increase the pressure so that the child makes a maximum of decisions at his particular age and maturity level. Older children should do the same for important events that they see, hear, or take part in. Show your interest in what they do when away from you by sparking discussion and getting them to evaluate and analyze it for you. This includes entertainment — theater, concerts, plays, parties, church, television and radio.

G. Provide the intellectual tools which your child can use in analyzing. These include definitions (freedom, responsibility, values, attitudes, democracy, or whatever the subject under discussion might be). Make sure your child understands the words you are using so that you will at least be speaking the same language. The value categories we use in this course, for example, are simply defined and may be used in every family.

1. *Power* (or influence), being listened to, the degree to which a person takes part in making important decisions that directly or indirectly affect him. Voting, for example, is an act of power. So is holding an office in a social, fraternal, educational or political organization. Also, speaking out on a problem or subject at a meeting or group.
2. *Respect* can be recognition, honor, admiration, the degree of discrimination against people or recognition of them in their capacity as human beings.
3. *Wealth* refers to the goods and services people need as well as want.
4. *Enlightenment* is the information one learns and needs to make any decision.
5. *Skill* is the development and use of one's native and acquired talents.
6. *Well-being* refers to one's mental and physical health (feeling).
7. *Rectitude* (or responsibility) refers to ones standards, ethics, sense of "right and wrong," responsibility, trustworthiness, honesty, justice.
8. *Affection* means love, friendship, loyalty, caring for and about people.

H. Situations *are created* which provide motivation or an inner desire to learn. These can be put in terms of values goals such as a need to be respected, the need to know (enlightenment), to acquire skills, to be

loved, to earn money, to be healthy, to help make
one's own decisions, and to be valued as a moral and
ethical person.

1. Motivation for learning is provided by parents
    who show *respect* for achievement in all areas
    regardless of degree. This includes handi-
    craft or projects wherever they may be done.
2. Children are motivated by showing them where
    to find answers to their own questions without
    the parent answering the questions for them.
    Children are motivated by the family providing
    opportunities for enlightenment such as trips to
    museums, art galleries, concerts, drama, field
    trips, films, radio and television stations or
    performances.
3. Children are motivated by showing them the
    need to acquire *skills* — to be able to read in
    order to learn about sports, hobbies, and fields
    of interest. How to write so as to communicate
    with friends. How to use numbers so as to keep
    scores and records for games, as well as to keep
    track of savings and expenditures. How to build
    things. To be able to get along with people and
    to be wanted by their own peers is also a basic
    motivation for gaining enlightenment in social
    skills.
4. Children are motivated to learn in order to be
    loved and respected so as to share interpersonal
    relations and to build their own friendships and
    ethical standards.
5. Children are motivated by the need to *earn
    money* (wealth). They need to change money
    and keep receipts of money and expenditures; to
    write well so as to get and keep jobs; to become
    enlightened so as to develop those personal traits
    that will make them better employees (and

eventually managers and executives), and citizens.

6. You can motivate your children to be physically and mentally *healthy* (Well-Being)in many ways. Tell them about diseases when you were a youngster or let them watch a western on television in which diseases from plague, smallpox, cholera, diptheria, chickenpox, T.B., pneumonia, mastoid, and many others carried off so many pioneers.

   Parents should carefully point out how "enlightenment" — scientific research and development — have virtually eliminated the epidemic character of many of these diseases during the last fifty years. Children should know why safety rules are for their personal benefit and why we have community health measures (restaurant inspection, water purification, malaria control, meat inspection, etc.).

7. Motivate children to make their own *decisions*. Discuss how you and your spouse make important decisions in your family. Include children in making decisions at home and explain why a decision is practical or impractical. Avoid if possible the "good" and "bad" designations.

8. Motivate your children to understand moral and ethical standards and the need for them. Discuss various types of standards and encourage your children to find their own reasons why a person should be honest, loyal, trustworthy, etc. Use examples in their own family and school life to show what happens when people violate standards of behavior.

WORKSHEET

1. How is the house built?

2. Why does water run out of the faucet.

3. Read a book or story and discuss why the characters did what they did.

4. Plan and take a trip to the fire station, police station, library, zoo, observatory, ocean tide pools, mountain forests and streams, grocery store, electric and sewer plants, airports, etc., etc.

5. Ask each child to answer (write) with your help:

   a. What do I know about milk? Bread? Eggs? Etc.

   b. What are clothes made out of? (kinds of materials: follow up with what is cotton? Wood? Nylon, Orlon, Polyester, etc.)

   c. Were clothes ever made of furs? What animals had furs that were used for clothes?

   d. Why do lights "turn on?"

   e. What is a budget? How does mother make up a food budget and what does she have to think about when she does?

f. (1) Name five kinds of appliances (small machines) we use at home.

(2) Why do we use electrical appliances?

(3) What did the invention of these do for mother at home? For father? For me?

g. Once people had to make up their own entertainment (play) at home. What has changed? Do you see how these change home lifestyles for the better? For the worse?

h. How does a washing machine work (clean clothes)? Indians use to do it by beating wet clothes against a rock — does the washing machine use part of the same principle?

6. Pick a series of incidents in which the whole family was involved and see how each taught you something about each other's values — affection, respect, well-being, skill, enlightenment, rectitude, power, wealth.

7. a. What motivating forces has each of your children already shown?

b. Indicate specifically how you are strengthening these motivations or helping your children to do so (*no generalizations please!*).

8. a. Since the home and family are major educational "resources" for children, what subjects or areas of enlightenment do you think are best taught in the home by parents?

b. Take each area in your answer (a) and show how you are or intend to handle each with your children. (Be specific or you'll miss the point of this exercise.)

9. Discuss: "Older or superior children can teach younger or other children effectively with parental help."

10. In order of importance as you now see them, what are the most important matters you learned at home from your parents and family?

Father

a.

b.

c.

d.

e.

Mother

a.

b.

c.

d.

e.

Skill

Definition: To provide opportunities at home and in the community for each child to discover and develop his talents to the limits of his potential ability.

A. Encouragement of each child to develop his talents and skills to his or her full capacity.

1. Motor Skills

   a. Each child should be encouraged to try various physical activities at home — skipping, jumping, running and other healthful forms of exercise.

      (1) Find time regularly (daily if possible) to comment or discuss the enjoyment (another word for "turning on") gained from these activities.

      (2) Encourage your child to talk about his recreation (exercise) and why he enjoys each part of it (the "why" and his understanding of it is the "key," so work on this even with the smallest children so they find the answer with you); avoid giving the answer, by drawing it from the youngster.

(3) Deliberately teach your child not only to be a leader in playing with other children, but also how to be one of the group and take instruction from other "leaders."

(4) Both mother and father should strive to take a part in their child's recreation — toss the ball, play games with them from ping pong to chess, basketball, picnicing, etc. Take some part in the activity so they see you as more than the provider, chef, housekeeper, breadwinner, or disciplinarian in their lives.

(5) Find ways to encourage the child who does not normally enter into healthful activity, and do it without making it a chore to the youngster. Find the right "turn on" button in the kind of activity that the child will and does enjoy (not just the ones you don't mind doing!)

(6) Get your older children to help plan and play with the younger ones — help train them in the skills by making them "instructors" or assistant "coaches."

(7) Encourage each child to keep score (his own particularly), and to judge his own progress and set his own individual standards rather than to compete beyond his ability and skill. (Be sure and recognize his improvement, regardless of how small it may be, and do it each time.) If he/she wishes to be competitive, encourage healthy competition, and discourage strongly the "win at all costs" when playing with family and friends. En-

courage and emphasize "sportsmanship;" meet the "bad loser" problem positively.

b. Encourage older children to take active part in group and team type games and sports by providing time and opportunities, equipment and real instruction. (Examples: swimming, water polo, tennis, little league, pony league, "Pop" Warner football league, Girl and Boy Scouts, Camp Fire Girls, YMCA, scuba diving, city recreation (park and playground) teams, CYO, etc.).

(1) If boys and girls do not each have their own sets of equipment, make arrangements for sharing.

(2) Take advantage of the free or low cost city recreation sports training programs for young people; lessons are offered in many sport skills as well as handicrafts and hobbies. Select at least one that is a 10-12 month a year activity, and another that is intensively followed during summer vacations when time can hang heavily on a youngster's hands.

(3) Provide home time *every day* for play and outdoor sport activity when skill can be developed by practice or actual use. (Driveway basketball, sandlot baseball, tennis, swimming, etc.)

(4) Encourage each child to try more new skills before their interest in the old ones have completely dissipated.

(5) Encourage each child to move about and seek new teams when a season begins, so that he/she will broaden his/her range of friends and teammates.

c. Encourage at home those skills that a child will need throughout his whole life, even though they may be taught in school.

(1) Use every opportunity to help your child to develop writing and reading skills. Letters to Santa Claus, Grandmother, absent fathers, ill friends and such, teach writing skills simply and interestingly if properly handled. Leave notes on kitchen bulletin board for children to read. Encourage "pen pals," summer camp reports home that say more than "having fun, send money." Encourage use of city library (arrange time for children to go and select their own reading materials); subscribe to children's magazines (let them help select what they want to read); make books a part of family life. Instead of buying invitations to parties encourage children to design and make their own, using materials they help select.

(2) Encourage each child's interest in art and music starting at very early ages with art materials, pictures, records, etc. Take them to the free museums and showings. Make these part of an overall experience (picnic, lunch, etc.). Encourage your children to decorate their own rooms with their pictures and handiwork. Teach them design and feeling, poster making, and how to express themselves in color and form.

d. Provide opportunities for each child to develop skills in music (including social dancing for both boys and girls if not contrary to family beliefs).

(1) Singing and dancing is a natural outlet for man, and when encouraged can become a satisfying "turn on" for many young people. There are many choral groups and choirs and dance groups for young people which contribute to personal skills as well as social skills.

(2) When special musical interest or talent is shown take positive steps to encourage and develop it.

(3) Encourage children to write their own songs and to select music for special occasions – parties, dinners, etc.

(4) Children who show little talent in music should not be "turned off" by discouraging them or being told to stop singing or playing, but should be led to use music as a fruitful and satisfying hobby; meanwhile strongly encourage them in the use of other talents.

e. Help each child – girl and boy – to learn how to use tools and machines which are used in everyday life.

(1) Hammer, saws, nails, screwdrivers, pliers, wrenches are essential to home life, and each child needs to perfect his knowledge and skill in home projects. Both girls and boys need knowledge of how to use properly scissors, knives, sewing machines, kitchen appliances, workshop tools, etc. Both parents should make positive efforts to have both sons and

daughters develop skills with these modern essentials.

(2) A part of home-teaching should be visits with father and mother to garages, farms, factories, etc., where children can see people using all manner of tools productively and with responsibility.

(3) Teach each child how to use the telephone responsibly – to call for help (fire, police, neighbor, relatives, and especially the doctor and operator). Emphasize telephone courtesy and competent communication skill.

(4) Home workshops for children are excellent skill developing areas. Besides use of tools and their care, the home instruction should include safety measures. This should include workshops for girls as well as boys.

(5) With young as well as older children use both *indoor* as well as *outdoor* skill development projects – basket weaving, pottery making, hot mat sewing, leathercraft, crocheting, embroidery, etc.

2. Thinking skills

    a. Home taught methods of solving problems.

        (1) Teach each child to identify and state his problem clearly, and to justify trying to solve them by answering the question "How will solving this problem help me or other people to achieve what I (or they) want?" *(This is the first step in learning to think systematically.)*

(2) Teach your child to "search" for accurate information on what happened in the past which has to do with his problem. *(Trend thinking.)*

(3) Help him/her develop information about what is happening at the present time that is pertinent to his/her problem. *(Condition thinking.)*

(4) Help the child to estimate or predict what could happen regarding his problem unless something is done to solve it. *(Projective thinking.)*

(5) Have the child make a complete list of all the ways he can think of for solving the problem. (This is the first step in *alternative thinking* and gives you a priceless opportunity to lead your child into the exciting experience of *creative thinking* about how his problem can be solved and *his* goals reached.)

(6) Help and allow the child to select which of the solutions seem most likely to solve the problem and to try them out in order to see which is the most effective in reaching the desired end. If none proves effective, have the child seek and appraise other alternatives that might be used to reach goal. (This is the major step in alternative thinking and problem solving — DECISION MAKING — the most often neglected responsibility by parents in raising their children. Much lip service is given to this need by parents, but all-too-often parents negate the result by refusing to follow through with the child and let him learn.)

(7) Encourage each child to solve his own individual problems. Offer guides and encouragement (even though you might find it easier and less time consuming to do the solving for the child). Don't automatically solve each problem every time your child comes to a roadblock; encourage him to find the way around it. Offer solutions but don't dictate one (and wherever you possibly can, live with the solution the child selects *unless it really is harmful or impossible)*. Remember, one learns responsibility only by being given responsibility for making his OWN decisions — even though sometimes it may lead to an error. We can, after all, learn from our mistakes and not get too badly hurt if mother or father is there to pick us up; but we learn little if every decision is made for us!

(8) Present family problems to your children to discuss, and help formulate alternatives or possible solutions. Including them in the family discussion and decision-making helps develop not only their sense of belonging, but their skills, as well as providing further confidence in making their own decisions.

3. Communication Skills

   a. Home taught methods of teaching children to communicate effectively.

      (1) Help your child to organize his thoughts and express them effectively.

      (2) Demonstrate to him that he must use different methods with each of his "aud-

iences." He communicates differently with his parents and brothers and sisters than with neighbors and other children, tradespeople, etc.

(3) Teach him how to analyze the effect he wants to achieve in communicating with each of his "audiences." What goals does he seek, how best to express them, what will "influence" others, etc.

(4) As a "communicator" teach him to be prepared to speak or write to the particular audience involved.

(5) Teach how to determine exactly what the "message" is he is trying to communicate without "burying" it so that his audience will miss the very point he wishes to establish. By practicing this at home he will become proficient in the simple techniques involved.

b. Teach children to become effective consumers of communication.

(1) Children are "prime consumers" of communication," and need to know what is really being said to them. For example, all forms of advertising use subtle methods to convey a message – hiding the real product-selling message behind a facade of pleasure or satisfaction-giving phrases or words or pictures.

(2) Teach children to recognize the characteristics of the communicator (his tone, his dress, his background, the "props" he uses, his deliberate appeal techniques, etc.)

(3) Teach children to recognize the "message" the communicator is trying to get

over to them regardless of how it is "dressed up" or emotionalized.

(4) Develop the ability of each of your children to appraise the true effect of the message upon them and others in the audience. (What is the communicator trying to get you to do? How? Why?)

(5) Help your child to become a good listener and a critical one. As soon as a conversation (TV advertisement, etc.) is finished ask your child to tell you exactly what was said, what was meant, and what effect it has on him. A Good Listener can become a very good communicator.

   (a) Play games that show the need for careful listening. (Stories, news articles, even the funny papers can be used for this.)

   (b) Have children interpret suggestions and reports made by others and to pre-determine what the results might be.

   (c) Parents set the example by listening carefully to each of their children.

(6) Help your child to interpret numbers; price tags, values of money and purchases at the store; estimate distances, weights, read simple graphs, charts and road maps.

4. Social skills (those involved in sharing human values with others).

   a. Introduce basic social skills at home — these should be deliberately taught and regularly checked until they are "second nature" for each child. Be sure and explain the "why," and how these are two-way streets, giving others respect and, through skill, receiving their respect.

(1) Teach them acceptable ways to make simple introductions to peers and adults as well as friends .

(2) Teach them proper telephone etiquette — how to answer the telephone, what can be properly said and what should not be.

(3) Instruct each child on how to await his turn in activities — to have patience and play the game according to the rules. Teach and have them practice "common courtesy."

(4) Discuss and demonstrate acceptable table manners, and explain why these are a mark of the well-bred child and why they are important in life.

(5) Teach children how to act when visitors come to their home.

b. Introduce courtesy as making it possible for people to get along in an orderly fashion without chaos and irritation.

(1) Teach youngsters how to make requests and express appreciation (without being perfunctory). "Please," "Thank You," "Excuse Me," "May I," etc.

(2) They must learn that friendliness and helpfulness beget friendliness and helpfulness, which in turn will make life more pleasurable and beneficial for them.

(3) Teach them to learn to accept gracefully the decision of the majority in the

family, among their friends, etc. Also how to accept decisions necessarily made by parents, teachers, neighbors, etc.

(4) Discuss cooperation as a "key" to family harmony and progress for each member.

(5) Illustrate how parents and children act in a democratic way toward each other as well as with other people.

5. Aesthetic skills ("The ability to enjoy or to create well-arranged patterns of form, color and sound which give beauty and pleasure to the individual and the family."). While some of the following is redundant, it needs to be re-emphasized, for it is in the arts that man develops his unique culture and humanness.

a. Children are deliberately and repeatedly introduced to art in broad spectrum.

(1) Art in the home — pictures, objects of art, etc.

(2) Children are taken to art exhibits and encouraged to look and discuss that which is shown in which they are interested.

(3) Children should be given opportunities to make their own evaluations of art (they will change with age and maturity), and exposed to the background of the artist and what his work shows about people and places.

(4) Encourage each child to get pleasure from the beauty of their environment as reflected in the sea, animals, mountains, plants, clouds, sunsets, storms, etc., including man-made designs and objects.

b. Introduce children to music very early and continue it throughout their lives at home.

c. Introduce children to "skill" literature: "how to" books, manuals, diagrams, maps, blue prints, hobby literature. Such literature will open doors to the whole world "of doing." Reading adventure literature ("moon walk" trips by astronauts, racing books, electronics, etc.) not only teaches skills but may be very motivating. The non-reading children may not like fiction accounts; scientific or "how to" literature in their interest areas may prove very interesting.

WORKSHEET

1. Call your city and/or county recreation and parks
    departments, and make a list of activities they offer
    that could interest your children. (Be sure and get
    exact dates and places.) Ask park officials to give
    you a precise list of public parks, their activities and
    facilities. Depending on age and maturity of each
    child discuss possible interests and encourage active
    participation. Working with each child separately,
    make a list of such activities which he/she can
    investigate after school, on weekends and during
    vacation.

    Note: In addition to individual and team sports,
    both recreation and park departments offer a wide
    variety of handicraft classes for younger and older
    children; teenagers, as well as adults. Some very
    important lifetime skills can be learned and de-
    veloped. Make a list of these and discuss them with
    your family.

2. Call your art museum and newspaper and put a list of "coming music, drama & art events" on the kitchen bulletin board — or refrigerator door! — where everyone can read and discuss which they would like to go to. (Many high schools and local colleges, as well as civic groups, parks and recreation departments present excellent cultural events at little or low cost during the year, and these not only provide enlightenment but excellent opportunities to motivate or develop individual skills.)

3. Some families have developed (appointed and rotated) a "family poet" and a "family troubadour." For some event each week each writes a short poem or composes a song and both are presented at a family dinner or meeting.

4. Make a family agreement that for Christmas or birthdays all presents are to be hand made by the family members. Set a reasonable cost limit and time schedule. A prize should be offered for the best idea and best made present. (Make sure to supply proper tools and sufficient supplies.)

5. Referring to Section 2. on *"Thinking Skills,"* try a case study of each and every one of the methods with one of your children and report the results. Remember your skill will also increase the more you use these methods.

6. From national magazines tear out large advertisements for (a) cigarettes, (b) a hair oil or shampoo; (c) a liquor; (d) a sleeping or cold remedy; (e) a tranquilizer; (f) an insurance company.

   Ask your child to look at the advertisement and tell what "message" it is really giving.

   . . . Is it selling the product? How?

   . . . Is it selling pleasure; relief from pain or anxiety; sex; escape from life's tensions or does it really help solve the problem?

   Teach your child to recognize just what is being "sold" by advertising, and its relationship to problem solving or decision making. You can also use newspaper, radio and T.V. advertisements to play this game. Remind children what the purpose of advertising is, and why they must carefully analyze all advertising so as not to be fooled.

7. Look around the house and see if your "library" includes "how to" books or literature of interest to both your girls and boys. Make a chart showing what "how to" — skill or hobby — magazines or books you have and get regularly for each of your reading age children. (This includes, of course, Girl Scout and Boy Scout manuals and merit badge pamphlets, instructions and booklets on model making — cars, planes, boats, motors, camping, etc. — sewing and stitchery, etc.)

Power

Definition: Power is the measurement of a person's participation and influence in the making of important decisions involving himself, his family and others. These are decisions that are sanctioned by the family, group and society. They are, therefore, expected to be lived up to by the family and group, and are enforced against those who would violate them.

Choice is also an important part of this category — the ability and freedom to make choices. (These are unsanctioned decisions.) Each person makes thousands of these which have important bearing on his future personal life but which may have little consequence to others. For example, as Dr. Rucker points out, the choice between whether to vacation in the mountains or at the seashore is not a sanctioned choice for the individual (although in a family situation it could be). "The important point to be remembered is that many people expect to take part freely in the power process, and their well-being status suffers if they do not."

Children must see the importance of decision making, and from their earliest years must be given wide opportunities to actually participate in the making of decisions. It must be impressed upon them that decisions in which they participate are to be enforced.

"Otherwise, children will come to see that power and respect are being withheld from them, and their well-being statuses will be consequently damaged."

Should this damage be ignored the child may feel that he does not measure up to what the family expects of him, and he may develop feelings of guilt which could permanently distort and restrict his relationships with other people. Here are some alternatives which the family can use to build a healthy feeling of "power" — the important sense of having a significant role in making important decisions involving himself and others.

A. Both boys and girls are encouraged by father and mother (and older children in the family) to actively participate in making important decisions affecting life in and with the family.

   1. Children help choose the responsibilities they will take within the family. In taking part in the decision they acknowledge a fair distribution (according to age, strength and ability) of chores and their role in the "sharing" experience.

   2. Together family members establish a routine to be followed so that desirable patterns of sharing with as few stresses as possible can develop, still permitting each member to share in making important decisions.

   3. Shared decisions can be made with reference to meals, entertainment, clothing, toys, parties, vacations, chores, friends, school matters, pets, music and art lessons, hobbies, sports, and many other daily matters. As children grow up the nature and importance of their decisions will increase, and parents will need to permit a wider range of decisions (helping in discussion and selection) and learning to "live with" their

children's decisions, whenever they are not dangerous to themselves or others.

4. Children are permitted to choose what they would like to do after completion of their assigned tasks at home.

5. Parents must be alert to the natural instinct of young children to have adults make decisions for them, thereby passing off responsibility which can only be learned by having and using it. No child learns the proper use of power unless he both has it and is called upon regularly to use it; similarly one acquires a sense of responsibility only by having to make decisions and assume responsibility for them. The earlier in life this process is started the better. Authorities point out that long before a first birthday this process can be started by knowledgeable parents.

B. Numerous opportunities are given family members to express their opinions and vote on important issues with which the family is concerned.

1. Father and mother emphasize the need for each child to "say what is on his mind" and "vote" if he wants to exercise his "power."

2. To do this, father and mother seek both sides of any question (enlightenment) or issue so that each member can vote from knowledge, not just emotion or "like and dislike."

3. Discipline problems should be carefully discussed so that all factors of causation and results can be clarified (preferably before punishment is assessed, although this may not always be possible or desirable).

4. Father can work with boys on selection of tools, camping and sporting equipment, outdoor work,

family and school relationships, activities, church matters, etc.

5. Mother can work with girls on decisions regarding clothes, house matters, dating, personal affairs, arts, church matters, etc.

6. Reversing the situation, father should also have time to develop both attitudes and decisions with girls and mother with the boys.

C. Children are "convicted" and punished for anti-social behavior only on the basis of factual evidence that can be substantiated without reasonable doubt. (Democracy at home is basic to the development of a democratic foundation for the future of each child!)

1. Parents should use every opportunity to determine responsibility or guilt by:

   a. Sight.

   b. Confession (voluntary!)

   c. Witnesses (reliable, in number; but don't encourage "squealing" or tattle-tailing). On the other hand, teach children their responsibility to answer your questions honestly for their own good and for the protection of the family, group and society. While it is difficult to teach respect for law under certain circumstances, children must learn early that they are "involved," that the safety of the group and society is superior to that of the individual; that cooperation with authority does not mean "finking," but responsibility. Remember both the concept of being an "accessory" if one has knowledge of a "crime" and fails to cooperate, while at the same time he has the constitutional right to take the "Fifth Amendment" for his own protection. Those are the rules we must play by!

2. Value deprivations include:

   a. Withdrawal of power (temporary suspension of privileges — *not rights*; home restriction; allowance, etc.).

   b. Withdrawal of rewards (non-participation in special events — parties, theater, camp, dances, trips, etc., etc.). There are a number of values included here.

3. Punishment rendered:

   a. "Standardize" the penalty for same violation where possible. The child should know the extent of the punishment or penalty that will be involved if the offense is repeated. Also other children in the family must know so that they can judge the fairness when applied to other members.

   b. Must always be objective — never in anger or fear.

   c. Must be for the anti-social act and not for the child! The child must learn to understand the difference. He is being punished for an act, a violation, not for himself.

4. Children must be encouraged not to accuse others until they have heard both sides of the story.

5. Children must discourage their brothers and sisters who constantly "snitch" on other family members for misdeeds.

6. Each child must be allowed to quietly explain, as calmly as possible, his side of any case when he is accused of an anti-social act.

7. Every child must be considered to be truthful until proved otherwise, but statements should be double-checked when possible. (This simply means that the child is not *automatically* termed a liar no matter how flagrant the matter may be.) (Parents must remember that all children lie on occasion, but if they are constantly accused of lying it will tend to develop a personality situation in which lying can become automatic to the child.)

8. When there is doubt that all the facts of the case are known, no conviction should be allowed and no punishment assessed.

9. No child should be made a scapegoat under any circumstances.

10. No child should be accused or convicted of an anti-social act solely on the basis that he has committed such acts before and might possibly have committed this one.

11. Older children in the family learn to look for reasons and causes behind actions, so that they can then help the younger ones to avoid offending in the future.

12. Children are taught to understand that penalties are not set up to hurt any child, but are necessary to maintain order in the family, school and society.

13. Children are brought to an understanding that the degree of punishment, or temporary deprivation of a value or values, must match the degree of seriousness of the act involved.

14. Each child must be taught to realize the importance of the power he exercises over his brothers, sisters, and peers (and to a certain extent in the adult world), and how to handle it carefully and wisely so as not to waste his influence or to deprive others.

D. Children are encouraged to use their powers of influence and persuasion constructively, by freely discussing and suggesting while listening and valuing what others say and suggest.

1. Children should be given the privilege of discussing any discipline (how and why) the parent feels is needed.

2. Children should discuss with parents emergency methods (physicians, fire, police, plumber, electrician, phone, parent's place of employment, nearest relatives, etc.). Parents should make sure such plans, phone numbers, etc., are available and discuss with each child his use of these. The function of the Bulletin Board in hall or kitchens should be emphasized.

3. "Hands to ourselves" rule.

4. "Hands off other's property" rule.

5. "Safety rules" at home, road, on way to school, etc.

6. Methods of securing modification or exceptions to rules should be clearly understood by all children.

E. Attitudes of children and parents against the concentration of power in the hands of any one or small group of people should be clear and discussed, so as to promote understanding of the importance of democratic principles.

1. Children must understand that they must attain maturity before they can fully control their lives, but that they have a "right to my say" even though father and/or mother must for their protection and welfare have the final say. This is not tyranny or autocratic but recognition of responsibility — some of which is transferred to a child each year as he grows up and matures.

2. Illustrate actual examples of poor results from unplanned activities, or those poorly planned without taking others into account.

3. Both increase and rotate responsibilities as children grow and demonstrate increased abilities and capacity.

4. Give children the jobs they are capable of fulfilling, and fix responsibility for their completion. (Sometimes young ones will want to do things they can't quite do effectively; try to go along with that portion they want to try, helping them, etc. Generally they will give it up if they can't cut it, but you may be surprised if you work a little with them to establish skills and confidence.)

5. Show consequences of apathy on the child's part at every opportunity which will illustrate failure to show interest in family affairs.

6. Give opportunity for the overall family decision to override decisions of a small pressure group made without reference to the majority.

7. Work on establishing overall family goals for the year and measure the degree of success, so each child can feel his part in achievements as well as his responsibility for not attaining goals.

WORKSHEET

1. Make a *list* of the decisions *you made* today *that directly affected other members* of the family (choice of meals, theater, clothes, chores, entertainment, car, house, vacation, etc., etc.). Check those you discussed *first* with spouse; double check those you made *after* discussing the alternatives with your children; put a "star" next to those you *could* have discussed with the children *but didn't.*

2. *Freedoms/Rights vs. Responsibilities.* **This is one of the important "keys," not only to family harmony and progress, but to individual growth, maturity and character development. Working directly with your children let each make an individual chart lining up his freedoms/rights with his responsibilities.**

John (11)

Rights/Freedoms	*Responsibilities*
1.	
2.	
3.	
etc., etc.	

3. *Parental Responsibility* ("**Parent Power vs. Youth Power**"). This follows No. 2 above naturally and should be done with each child and then discussed, as the opportunity arises, in a family conference. The objective here is to have each child separately list the responsibilities he/she acknowledges are those of mother and/or father. If he/she feels that he should "have a say" in any parental decision, have him spell out what limitations there should be, and to what extent his views should be accepted. If this exercise is sincerely developed, it should result in "closing the generation gap" (if any), and promote family understanding and harmony.

Wealth

Definition: To the young person "Wealth" applies to the "things" and services he needs and wants in his everyday life. Very early the feeling of "economic security" arises in each youth, and refers to the degree of goods and services he feels he requires to maintain a desirable standard of living at the moment and, as he matures, for the future.

CONCEPT: It is important for each child to learn that wealth is to be sought as an instrumental goal, or as a *base value,* from which other *scope* values can be gained, for with the increase in wealth the individual gains accessibility to many other value goals which depend upon the expenditure of his increases in wealth. With increases in his allowance, for example, he can afford sweets, the theater, a trip, a new dress, bathing suit, scuba equipment, tuition to college, books to enhance his enlightenment as well as well-being. Thus his other values — respect, skill, enlightenment, wealth itself, and well-being — "scope values," can be increased throughout his life. Wealth is often used as a base value to attain certain scope value benefits such as power and respect.

Money itself should be thought of as wealth only in that it represents a claim against society, a claim upon the goods and services of society.

While economic security would seem a value goal in which few children at the elementary school level are as yet interested, it is a highly important deferred goal which every child will inevitably be seeking during most of his lifetime. It is, therefore, in this area that we should begin as early as possible to condition his thinking by providing those experiences and practices that will help him to build his attitudes as well as skills and enlightenment — emphasizing, of course, the need for considering the freedom of choice and value assets of others.

A. From early age, parents should introduce their children to many of the occupations followed by friends, relatives, neighbors and other interesting people. How people earn a living should become an important part of home education.

   1. Parents can discuss their jobs — training and preparation, gains and rewards (emphasize the human inter-relationships as well as financial), opportunities for advancement, skills and other pluses.

   2. Discussion of life style and life goals should start early, for these will explain to young people why some parents spend long periods in preparing for future occupations which will produce the "wealth" they will need — to provide for their children, their welfare and education as well as parent needs and wants.

   3. Encourage the exchange of similar information and discussions with neighbors, friends and relatives and your children.

   4. It is essential to point out the handicaps of certain types of occupations, their "dead end" factor, and the problems involved. While the "glamour" of each occupation will become

evident, each child should learn of the routine involved, the hard effort required to succeed.

B. Parents provide the opportunities for young people to "explore" other occupations and jobs available in the community.

1. Besides the occupations of friends, neighbors and relatives, young people should have the opportunity on a planned (but *not* necessarily routinized) basis to explore the business and industries, services and professions in their own community. This goal is readily realized by both parents taking advantage of normal opportunities: taking young people to market and in the course of buying point out the wide variety of roles played by the employees – buying, storing, inventory, marking and labeling, pricing, grading, displaying, cashiering, and managing. Visits to the drug store, the service station and garage, a farm or ranch, dairy, cannery, museum, park, courts, police and fire stations, mayor's office, city council, school board, construction sites, doctor and dentist offices, hospitals, laboratories, forest and ranger services (county, state and federal parks); lumber, sugar, flour mills, cement plants, and many other places offer ample opportunities throughout the child's informative years to give him a broad understanding of the great depth of opportunities and occupational satisfactions available to young men and women.

2. Books, magazines and newspapers, radio, and television can be excellently programmed to contribute to a boy's or girl's appreciation of many traditional occupations (even horse shoeing where the income is now from $15,000

to $20,000 a year in many states, particularly California, and where classes in major universities offering such instruction are over-filled annually) and many new ones (space, nuclear energy, oceanography, etc.). The point here is that parents use these opportunities to call attention to facts and needs rather than have the young reader, listener or viewer pass over the pertinent factors in their interest in *what* is being done. (Example: the long educational training to be a doctor, lawyer, astronauts, their secondary period of internship or acquiring experience, their physical and mental conditioning are generally overlooked in watching them win a sensational trial, perform a delicate heart operation, or walk on the moon.) Parents should be aware of the great mass of *free* material that they (or preferably their children) can write for and obtain on almost any profession, trade, or other activity. (Consult your community librarian, school librarian, or officials of these organizations.

C. Children should be encouraged to "play" at and imitate the kinds of occupations they may — for the moment at least — find interesting.

1. Playing doctor and nurse, teacher, "cops," border patrolman, soldier, sailor, storekeeper, chemist, etc., can be highly constructive and attitude-developing. Without structuring the child's role-playing, parents can contribute to the "gains" from such playing by casually providing "doctor" and "nurse" kits; badges and fingerprinting sets along with "detective" games involving excellent memory developers — such as looking at a picture for ten seconds and then trying to remember as many items in the picture

as possible, or a store window, or identifying makes of cars or license plates by states, symbols, etc., either while at home or while driving with the family.

2. Photographs and booklets which will interest the younger as well as older children can be obtained — many free or at very little expense — for the young person to decorate his own room, den or play area. Never before have these been available in such quantity and in such quality (large and in color). Children and young people are frequently embarrassed to write for such items, and in this parents can help by assisting the youth in writing and mailing his request and suggesting places where he can obtain the materials.

3. Making "occupation" cutouts from newspapers, magazines, etc., can be highly interesting and profitable conditioning fun on days when the weather is inclement or for some other reason outside play is not feasible or desirable.

D. Children should be educated at home by parents on accepting assignments (chores), developing pride and responsibility for their work and what it takes to get and keep a job.

1. Working to provide one's needs and wants (wealth) is a developing trait, and requires parent patience and diligence if youngsters are to acquire motivation and effective work attitudes and habits. Young people just do not acquire these automatically; they are acquired only after long and continuous efforts by parents and their children. Unless these start *before* school age and continue throughout youth, there will be measurable delay in the

development of responsibility and even decision making.

a. Through older brothers, sisters, and friends, as well as adults, children learn what part-time jobs are available in their community that suit their age and abilities.

b. "Chores" around the home are divided into those which are their *responsibility* as part of a family group, and those extra for which some pre-determined remuneration may be expected. There should be both kinds as early in life as a child can do them (even though the "remuneration" be of the penny and nickel variety; for example: a child doesn't get paid for care of his room or taking out the garbage, but he could receive money for picking up nails and broken glass in an alley, the street or vacant lot next door. Many parents have lawn and garden work as part of "family chores," but washing and polishing the car as a "remunerated job." There is no hard or fast rule here, but parents would be well-advised to make such divisions early and to encourage the acquisition of wealth (needs and wants other than those normally supplied). Youngsters could earn their own money for candy, shows, etc.

c. Parents should casually discuss and analyze how young people can apply for jobs (the "proper approach" technique). This would include speech, dress, time, and other factors which employers would expect.

d. Parents might discuss what things a young person should avoid when applying for a job and in holding one. Let the young person help make a list of the things he would expect of a worker if he hired one: promptness, courtesy, appearance, etc. Assist the youth to make his list realistic. Discuss why many employers just will not employ people who appear in hippie-type clothes, hair and adornment.

2. Parents should help their children to study the requirements for obtaining and holding a permanent job. A start on such discussions should probably be made while the youngster is in grade school. Concepts and attitudes are more easily accepted and formed at an earlier age, than waiting until as a teen-ager he/she "suddenly" finds that it's a "work-a-day world," and few of us are born with a silver spoon in our mouths that will carry us throughout our adult lives!

a. Emphasis on "the American Way" should start early. Competition is still the spice of life, and each child must learn the dignity of gaining by his own efforts; that "gains" rightfully are or should be in proportion to his own efforts; that "profit" is not only highly desirable, but makes it possible to increase one's wealth as well as to increase one's service to others — family, friends, relatives, city, state and nation.

b. Family discussion on "What do I owe my employer?" should be semi-routine along with the idea of "What do I owe my employee?" Father and mother's jobs or occupations should make good examples. Why does Dad put in overtime? Why does he bring "home work" from the office to work on at night? Why does he go back to the store to finish some task after dinner?

    c. Great emphasis should be placed on the gains and rewards from a job "well done," not just the monetary gains but the personal gains and satisfactions. Parents should point out the relationship between the ability to "buy" fun and pleasure as related to the job, and the earning of money to supply these "wants."

E. Young people should be given instruction and the opportunity to secure goods and services for themselves.

    1. They investigate how goods are distributed even though not produced in their own community.

        a. Discuss the "obvious" (to adults but NOT always to young people) of how we can eat tomatoes (corn-on-the-cob, etc.) 12 months a year even though not grown here for 6 months out of the year. Explain how production must be keyed to distribution and sales to make an overall economy. (Include transportation and the importance of railroads, trucks, etc.; selling techniques so we all can get what is produced; the increase in jobs for everyone who wants to work if he takes advantage of the opportunity and time while young to get properly trained or to acquire skills and knowledge.)

        b. Children find out who produces the products they use (show them the labels in the market with cans of substances from Korea, Taiwan, Japan, Germany, etc., etc., as well as from almost every state). Do the same in clothing stores, etc.

    2. Help youngsters to understand buying and sell-

ing in relation to quality and prices. Parents have a far better opportunity to do this than does the school, *if* they make a habit of taking children to market and shopping.

    a. They learn why stores ask different prices for similar materials.

    b. They learn why certain materials are warmer or cooler than others.

    c. They learn what the significance of a label is.

    d. They study advertisements and become discerning about them.

    e. They learn to make their own choices when buying similar items of different quality (and in accord with their ability to buy).

3. Children practice managing their money (and responsibility in using other people's funds — mother's if sent to the store, etc.).

    a. Children pay for lunches and keep account of money.

    b. Children learn thrift and the reasons for it when setting up and adding to their own bank (savings) accounts.

    c. Young people help plan the spending of limited funds when they take part in setting up family picnics, outings, vacations, etc.

    d. They can be taught by parents to analyze and make use of savings and budgeting systems.

F. Children and young adults are encouraged by family discussions to oppose all kinds of job discrimination for reasons other than merit. (Gear such discussions to the maturity level of your children.)

1. Young people — friends, neighbors and peers — are not discriminated against because of their wealth or lack of it.

2. Young people are taught not to select others for honors and offices on the basis of *their family's* economic or social status.

3. Parents discuss why some students may not be able to donate or contribute to drives, collections, etc.

4. Children are taught that some students or friends, and in some instances, they, cannot buy expensive costumes, materials, or take part in costly projects or activities. Parents must learn how to teach young people to recognize their financial limitations and, for the good of the whole family, not to feel so deprived that they contribute to family upset and problems.

5. Cleanliness, neatness and simplicity in appearance rather than ostentation are stressed more than the quality or quantity of clothes owned.

6. Families should impress upon children that the major function of the individual engaged in an occupation or profession is to provide the goods and/or services required by this society in promoting the wider distribution of human values. *They must emphasize that the creation of wealth is not an end in itself, but rather a means to the realization of human potentials in all the value categories.*

WORKSHEET

1. Have your children prepare a list (or plan a family discussion) of all the occupations represented by members of the family: father, mother, uncles, aunts, grandfathers, older brothers and sisters (you can also use friends and neighbors in a second list). After each job or occupation help them make a series of value judgements as to (a) which jobs provide the relative with the most "goods and services" *now,* (b) the potential for the future in the job (both in income-wealth and advancement which would mean more income), (c) the amount of training (years of apprenticeship, cost, education) needed for each job, (d) the amount of equipment and energy (machinery, horsepower, manpower) each job commands (has).

2. Explain wealth, poverty, unemployment, capitalism, socialism, communism (in economic sense) to your children. Drive them through the slums, tenements and impoverished areas. Discuss what you see about lifestyles, the despair of people, what becomes of these people who have exactly the same basic needs and wants (values) as more fortunate people. Explain what is and can be done to help these people and eradicate this social (economic) blight. You can explain this to even small children, explaining why other children have different clothes and fewer toys, food, etc.

3. Have each young person make a monthly schedule of his "needs" and "wants" – his "budget" – first, listing each need: clothing, lunch money, club dues, etc. Second, listing each want: candy, entertainment, hobby materials, etc. (Don't forget school costs, theater, Disneyland, zoo, scouts, YMCA, pets, transportation, etc.) Thirdly, list "income," money to be received for doing specific agreed upon tasks or jobs. Fourthly, show how much subsidy (allowance) parents are going to have to give to "balance" the account.

Well-Being

Definition: The attainment and maintenance of a high degree of mental and physical health.

Well-being, as Dr. Rucker (and others) so clearly shows, is of special importance in a democratic society which depends upon a continuing process of creative and productive activity for its growth and maintenance. To validate such an observation one needs only recall those places and times during the past half-century where serious value deprivations resulted in a widespread lower well-being of whole nations, with accompanying fears and tensions that proved the greatest block to their creative and productive activity.

Serious, prolonged, or unresolved deprivations in any of the categories of values inevitably result in mental ill-health (and not infrequently, in physical ill-health). As pointed out so often, every man, woman, and child without exception has basic needs in each of the value categories: affection, respect, wealth (goods and services), enlightenment, skill, power (influence), well-being, and rectitude (responsibility). Ongoing research with young people this past decade clearly indicates that one of the most critical problems facing this nation is the great number of children who suffer from deprivation of well-being, with its consequent distortion of their present and possibly future creative and productive capacities.

Well-being is more than a state of being; it is also an important state of mind. It is characterized not only by good health (the lack of physical illness), and feeling fit, but by happiness and contentment. It includes a recognition and acceptance of one's physical and mental limitations, and the frank realization that every person has different capabilities. Parents must be aware that over-indulgence in any of the values may result in a serious deprivation in well-being (among other categories, as well), which may trigger unacceptable coping behaviors. An important goal of the family, therefore, is to create and maintain a home environment most conducive to maximization of each child's values; one that provides the all-important foundation for both mental health and achievement (including that in school!) and physical well-being.

A. Parents should teach (and practice) the principles and provide the safeguards of good physical and mental health geared specifically to the age, maturity and capabilities of each child.

   1. Home environment should be planned so as to be conducive to good physical and mental health.

      a. House designs should be planned or renovated with children in mind so as to build in low cost conveniences for toddlers and growing children, and provide safeguards against dangerous areas and items (doors, window checks, one-way internal nursery windows, ventilation, lights, dimmer lights, ramps along with safety steps, check locks on basement (cellar) and attic doors, expanding gates at top and bottom of stairs; heater protectors, stove and appliance protection, bathroom fixture guards and arrangement for small children, yard fencing, driveway protection, non-poisonous planting, etc., etc.).

b. Children should be aware of proper ventilation and lighting in the home, with special attention devoted to reading and study areas.

c. Children's furniture — tables, chairs, stools, beds, bathinettes, playpens, dressers, toilet chairs, wardrobes, etc. — should be designed and purchased with safety in mind. Top-heaviness, ease of turning or pulling over, sharp corners, higher or lower than necessary, head-catching slot areas, poison paints, etc., are easily identifiable hazards readily avoided.

d. Play areas call for safety checks as well as utility of design. Swings, barrels, room and equipment corners, electric fixtures and cords, toys, padding (rugs, sod or other play area or yard surfacing) should be part of parent concern daily.

2. Planning and implementing a regular health program to meet children's needs.

a. Complete physical examinations for each child including eye, ear, nose, throat, blood, teeth, gums, feet, sex organs, hair and scalp, etc.) with such lab work as the physician recommends — not just a cursory "once over." Take advantage of the astonishing progress in preventative medicine including all vaccinations and innoculations! As never before, "an ounce of prevention is worth more than a pound of cure."

b. Food habits also influence the mental health of your children. Plan healthful, balanced diets, avoid food fads. Nutrition experts are available to every family at little or no cost. Use them and follow their and your physician's advice. You don't have to be rich to eat well, but you do have to know what to eat, how to prepare it and when to eat it. How you feed your child may not only influence his personality, his health, his success in life but, also how long he may live.

c. Schedule regular dental and vision checks — and *don't* depend just on those given infrequently in schools!

d. Be alert to signs of "something wrong" — loss of appetite, runny nose, sore spots, bleeding, loss of energy, limping, sleeplessness or continual sleepiness, fever, unusual irritability, fainting, etc., etc. Be concerned, but don't transfer it to your child!

e. Don't "dose" children except on advice of a physician! Even aspirin can have unpleasant side effects. Discuss on-going medication with your doctor first . . . it may be too late when trouble results.

f. Teach good health habits at home starting at infancy   care of teeth, use of face tissues or handkerchief, covering mouth when sneezing or coughing, washing hands before eating and after using bathroom, proper diet, and proper clothes.

g. Plan sound, wholesome sex education beginning with the very young so that it is a natural growth. Avoid making it a "big thing," but be scrupulously honest and don't "duck" the tough or embarrassing questions with that timeless cop-out, "you're too young," or "you don't need to know that now," or "someday when you're a big boy, Daddy will tell you all about that!" Remember: "If they are old enough to ask (or otherwise evince an interest), they are old enough to be told." One simple question, however, *need not* bring on a full course answer *unless* it is obviously time for it.

h. Frequent "suspicious" illnesses should be carefully analyzed. They may indicate a deprivation felt by the child in any of the other value categories and should be checked. Example: a child regularly complaining of a headache, or a pain in the stomach can be simply saying, "I want (need) someone to pay attention (affection) to me." Generally speaking, the ploy works and he/she will repeat the pattern whenever the deprivation is felt. School problems can cause home problems and visa versa.

B. Mental health requires serious and consistent parent alertness.

1. Continual parent attention is needed to help children develop a sense of self-respect (self-esteem) and self-responsibility, both of which have strong mental health influence.

a. Children cannot develop a lasting sense of self-respect without being given the opportunity to develop responsibility. They can only develop responsibility by being given responsibility commensurate with their abilities, and maturity. Ideally this training should begin in infancy.

b. Responsibility should also be linked to consequences for fulfilling them as well as not meeting them. Avoid "looking the other way" or ignoring failure to fulfill the responsibility. *Be consistent!!* Let each child know the limits of his responsibility, as he will find security in this.

c. Encourage each child to accept responsibility for his own behavior. Help him to identify and check out alternatives and consequences before he acts in any given situation. Instead of "Why did you do that?" try asking, "Can you think of other ways you might have done it?" Adhere to the rules you and the children discuss and agree on. Avoid accepting excuses; it is quite normal for young people to see how far they can go with each parent.

d. Consistency, fairness and calmness (in spite of strong provocation) should be the practiced goal of each parent at all times. Each contributes to the mental health of the child *as well as that of the parent.*

e. Resolve disputes or problems in such a manner that neither the child nor parent feels he is always the "loser."

f. Build self-confidence by seeing that the child frequently knows the feeling of success. Success is the stuff we grow on, while repeated failures inhibit us and destroy our confidence. Failure also destroys the child's sense of responsibility, and leads to loss of initiative, willingness to follow others often without reason, and cow-like acceptance of "stronger" (though often aberrant) peer leadership or direction. Alienation often results, evidenced many times by emotional disturbances or mental illness.

g. Help children and young people to resolve inner tensions that rob them of peace-of-mind, contentment and happiness. If not relieved, such tensions can lead to violent and otherwise unacceptable behavior. Learning to adequately cope with his own problems in a positive way also prepares youth to cope with the larger problems in the world about him.

h. Give each child responsibility, let him practice it (and parents should learn to live with his stumbling and imperfect performance while he is building up his confidence, skill and degree of responsibility).

i. Be alert for signs of loneliness, alienation (few friends and no desire to make them), suspicion, strong and sometimes uncontrolled bursts of aggressive behavior, hate, prolonged crying and unhappiness.

2. Let children know you are *sincerely interested* in their activities.

a. Participation in community, school, church, youth organizations can not only build skill and enlightenment values, but well-being in that it helps use excess energies. While it may not be always true, it is obvious that a child voluntarily occupied with continual interesting healthful activities (thus avoiding boredom) will be less likely to get into trouble.

b. Does your child always want to go over to another child's house to play? Or, does he bring or attract others to your home? If the former, you might analyze the situation at your home. Children should also like to share their own home environment; if they don't, you are being told something very important needs readjusting. Allow your children to visit and play with others, but remind them that "visitors" are expected to accept that home's rules.

c. Always know where young children are, and let them know that permission to "go out and play" or visit other children depends on their letting you know exactly where they are. Explain carefully that not only is this a rule of courtesy ("respect"), but of safety (their "well-being"). It also is a matter of the child's responsibility, and shares "well-being" with his parents. Then, extend them the same courtesy — let them know where you are at all times!!

d. While showing a definite interest in your child's activity, don't try (or insist) on being a part of everything he does! To do so contributes to dependency feelings, lack of confidence, possible alienation later, emotional and mental troubles.

e. Be careful about "pushing" your sports, hobbies, cultural ambitions (music, art, drama, dancing) on your children. Offer opportunities to see a wide variety of such activities. If the child shows real interest in any, open the door to opportunity, but don't let your avidness build up the child's reluctance or distaste for such activities. Some boys just don't like the sting of a baseball (and it builds up far-reaching fears if Dad becomes insistent). Some girls don't have the talent to become divas or prima ballerinas. Don't rush such interest before the child is *both* physically and mentally ready to participate. Pushing too hard and too fast can have a marked adverse effect on the child's sense of well-being – on his mental as well as physical well-being.

C. Well-being – happiness, contentment, an optimistic and eager attitude, an avid desire to participate actively – is particularly influenced by deprivations and enhancements of each and all of the other value categories. In turn, well-being greatly influences each of the other value categories. Thus, all of the categories are inter-dependent. Each of us has the need and want of all of them. Our mental as well as physical health throughout life – from infancy to old age – is dependent on successfully satisfying these values. How your children fare largely is dependent on you *now* . . . and, because of the long term effects of childhood, "now" may well influence them all the rest of their lives. And *that* is your responsibility ("rectitude").

HOME WORKSHOP

A. A FAMILY CHECK LIST ON "WELL-BEING"

First: Take time to sit down together (alone!) and briefly list the things you feel are important to your child's (each individual child) *well-being.* (Two columns for each child — (1) Physical well-being; and (2) Mental well-being. (Remember: if you do this carefully concentrating on each child, you will find your lists differ for each one!)

Second: Ask each child to list: (1) The things that make him *feel healthy*, and (2) The things that make him *feel happy.*

Third: With all family members present (so you can work together to add or change the lists), compare the similarities and differences in Parent and Child lists. Discuss these but avoid confrontations whenever possible.

Because of age, maturity, or insight, some of *your* goals *as parents* for each child's *well-being* may not be *valued* by him, consequently they may not add to *his* well-being. Here your ability as a "teacher-parent" can be used to build understanding, co-operation, compromise or acceptance. Don't take anything for granted, but plan and work on each problem area, remembering always to "push easy."

B. ENHANCING YOUR CHILD'S WELL-BEING

1. Discuss briefly with your spouse, three actual incidents that could have (or may have) jeopardized your child's well-being (health, happiness, or contentment) during the past week, and for each describe the "warning signs" (verbal clues or "body language") that made you aware of each situation. Carefully do this for each child.

2. Discuss with your spouse how each of these might be reduced or avoided in the future through using your new "awareness."

Rectitude

Definition: ". . . The personal recognition and individual commitment to such standards and ethics as will enable a person to develop, within the broad limits of his own and society's needs, an abiding sense of responsibility for his own attitudes and behavior – a dedication to truth, honesty, justice, fairness and compassion."

Rectitude involves a continually changing dualism . . . the perspective from which an evolving society views its citizens, and that from which the maturing individual views society. In a democracy – where responsible freedom is the ideal – the ever-broadening sharing of human values must be the constant goal. Such a society can only succeed when its many parts – the individual, *the family,* the school, the churches, the state, businesses and corporations, etc. – share in the ideal, and strive to reach the goal by practicing "sharing" within the framework of standards and ethics that are developed, approved and freely accepted by an overwhelming majority of its citizenry.

Conversely, whenever a strong or militant minority is, or feels it is, prevented from sharing in the development of its society's standards and ethics, and neither approves or accepts them as its lifestyle guides, the degree of non-sharing is quickly reflected in "non-responsible" behavior, a rapid decline in standards and ethics – a marked failure of rectitude! Chaos, lawlessness, violence, alienation of large and significant groups of people – notably the young and minority groups – inevitably result. Society and democracy cannot survive in such an environment. Repression and dictatorship then are inevitable.

In an "open" or democratic society in which each one of us quite naturally seeks to actualize his own potentialities, to secure the maximum blessings from personal liberty and opportunity, each must accept personal responsibility for seeing that others – especially our children – have continuing opportunity to fulfill their basic needs and wants in each of the categories of human values (Affection, Respect, Well-Being, Power, Wealth, Skill, Enlightenment and Rectitude.)

This places on parents (and on community leaders) initial and direct responsibility for the creation and use of sound and consistently applied techniques and strategies, designed to develop standards and ethics that are understandable and generally acceptable to all members of the family, relatives, friends and acquaintances.

It is obvious, therefore, that an individual's status of rectitude – the degree of moral practices and ethical standards *that he actually lives* – depends upon the degree to which he learns and assumes personal responsibility for, and contributes to, the shaping and sharing of basic human values.

Parents have a difficult task in establishing rectitude in a family. Dishonesty, cheating, lying, unfairness and injustice by either or both parents is quickly noted by even the very young. When asked, for example, if she knew she should not lie, a kindergartener quipped, "Well, my mother does! When Mrs. Blank called last Sunday, mother told me to tell her she wasn't home!"

Young Jimmy in the 4th grade said he thought his father didn't care much for the law or for policemen. "When we go for a ride, Daddy asks me to keep an eye out the back window, and let him know if I see a motorcycle cop come around the corner." A chick little second grader quipped on a TV show, "The lady gave my mother change for five dollars instead of for a dollar. Mother said it served her right for being so dumb, and put it away in her purse." Examples of child-recognized unfairness and injustice, humorous and tragic, are legion. It is difficult, however, to see how parents can expect children to learn and practice rectitude unless it is the lifestyle at home.

One last factor: learning rectitude requires "time" — time which some parents find galling. There are no really effective shortcuts to taking time (sometimes over and over again!) to sit down, and quietly (no shouting or screaming if you *really* want to be effective) talk over behavior and its many problems (standards, ethics, etc.) with your child(ren). To the exasperated parent who demands "How often do I have to go over this before I bat him in the head," there can be but one answer, "As often as necessary." For batting him in the head seldom cures the problem, at best it only inhibits the child from repeating the behavior *when he is in your presence!* The effective "cure" usually comes from understanding, patience and consistency — that is, "time" and your effective use of it. So . . . take time (and be a "model" of rectitude yourself)!

Children, as well as most adults, quickly learn the need for rules and ordered behavior in order to avoid confusion, misunderstanding, alienation, and often utter (and frightening) chaos. This section — which parallels that on "Rectitude" as applicable in schools given in *Human Values in Education* by Drs. Rucker, Arnspiger and Brodbeck, pages 70-78 — seeks to provide you, the parent, with guidelines to help meet your child's needs for standards and ethics that will meet his needs for stability in his life.

A. Your children are given every encouragement to establish their own moral standards above the minimum levels of prescribed rules and regulations.

   1. With your help young people of all ages learn and arrive at decisions relative to their personal obligations to constituted authority.

      a. Following discussion concerning maturation — and arriving at an understanding of why young people need help and protection as they grow from early childhood through adolescence if they are to survive in a world filled with very real dangers and obstacles — each child learns in what situations parents, teachers and other adults expect obedience. Once beyond the infant stage, the reasoning process *must* be used so that there is understanding by the child; patience and calmness will be required if he is to develop a clear understanding and to accept the "why."

      b. Children and young people need to learn in which areas parents and other adults should have more mature judgement than they can be expected to have, and therefore be able to offer protection or "smoother roads" to assist the young person. To even the youngest children, parents can easily demonstrate by a visit to the local zoo or to a neighboring farm, how all of nature's creatures advance through this parent protection period in which the young are taught acceptable behavioral patterns ("standards"), not only for their own survival and welfare, but for the tranquility and protection of all members of the family.

c. Young people are carefully taught their own physical and mental limitations, so that they come to know those situations in which they can rely on *personal judgement* ("decision-making") in making up their own minds.

d. Children learn why there must be some specific family and home regulations and why the well-being of the entire family unit depends upon complying with these.

(1) Through discussion or explanation they learn their responsibilities for sharing home tasks.

(2) Through detailed explanation and demonstration they learn how to act in family and home emergencies (fire, injury, explosion, illness, flood, etc.); emphasis is placed on the "responsibility to act," and then training and skill in acting. (Simulation and actual practice should be a part of the training where practical. Visits to the police and fire departments, hospitals, first aid training, and emergency telephoning should be a part of every child's experience during this training.)

(3) Families have specific tasks, house rules and house regulations, which, *after* discussion and full explanation, can be posted so that there can be no misunderstanding. These are amended as needed, exceptions allowed when desirable or essential, and are always open to further discussion and change as youngsters ma-

ture and are able to assume more responsibility in making their own decisions. They are not considered as changed, however, until they are expressly agreed upon, worded and posted when and where desirable (kitchen or room bulletin boards, etc.). Parents must "teach" by example and explanation the truism that "we are a government of laws (rules and regulations), not of men's whims or improvised notions." The family, of necessity, is a small governmental unit that avoids chaos and disaster through reasonable standards and rules.

e. Children learn what "leadership" responsibilities are carried by each member of the family. Parents must plan to provide each child with an opportunity to "lead" in something that is meaningful to each child. The importance of this becomes evident with each passing year in a child's development. He must learn how to lead, and that he is personally responsible in those instances where he voluntarily or by assignment undertakes to lead.

f. Children learn from each parent what authority is vested in adult neighbors, owners or operators of stores, of property near or in which they play, in parents of other children, and why. This must not be a perfunctory knowledge but needs repetitive discussion and understanding, to the point where the child uses such knowledge to develop attitudes, values and standards relative to other adults with whom he is to be in constant contact.

2. Children come to understand and react to family mores, customs and traditions as well as to those of their community, state and nation.

   a. Each child (individual attention!) is assisted by *each parent* to resolve his conflicts with family members, playmates, adults, etc., based on home standards as well as community and school standards. (Emphasis here must be on why "society" cannot survive complete individual freedom to the point where one person infringes on the rights and privileges of another or the group! Use actual examples taken from home or school which pinpoint the problem and the reasoning.)

     (1) When children act contrary to rules, regulations or acceptable standards, they must be taken aside and given sympathetic and patient explanation. Whenever possible explain penalty or punishment as *related to the deed,* not to love and affection for the child. (This SHOULD precede the imposition of penalty or punishment.)

     (2) There must be patient and reinforcing discussion from time to time as to why there are different standards among families, races, creeds, nations, etc. But in doing so it should be emphasized that individual "goals" (the "valuing categories") are the same for all peoples, and have been throughout history.

     (3) Through mutual discussion and individual as well as group (family, parents) encouragement, children help each

other to set their own high standards of behavior and to be able to explain what each standard is and why they believe in it.

b. Children learn how to react to conflicts with their "gang's standards," while still maintaining the standards which their conscience and experience tells them they should. (These should be constantly discussed at home. Parents should explain why it is frequently not desirable to "compete" with what "the other kids are doing," to become stereotyped and even conformists in the current fads that run counter not only to what the culture expects, but to what is personally best for him: for example, the very great difficulty being encountered by the "hippie" types in finding satisfactory employment and social acceptance.

   (1) There should be informed and low-keyed discussions on why certain differences in life-styles exist and why they run into difficulty. (What "values" deprivations are being manifested? Why are certain "alternatives" unacceptable?)

   (2) Discuss with your children how the gang's code of conduct may actually be not for the benefit of the whole gang, but for certain elements in the group — the leaders, the boys vis-a-vis the girls; the younger as against the older; etc. Discuss how a gang's "code" or standards can affect the life of their brothers and sisters as well as parents — to the detriment of all.

3. Young people set their own guides to action.

    a. Realizing that there will be numerous "back-slidings," each child at an early age should be given every *opportunity* to set his own standard of behavior.

        (1) Encourage trust and honesty by giving responsibility early for handling money and property belonging to other family members. (Shopping, etc.)

        (2) Through private conversations the mother or father (or both) attempt to assist children to reconcile conflicts in their standards.

        (3) Children should have the chance to make promises and to keep them.

        (4) Children should get experience in changing plans to meet the needs and circumstances of others (here again, discussion, patience and understanding by both parents are required).

        (5) Children learn (with help from both parents) to analyze situations which require the making of important choices, in order to discover what values are involved. This requires frequent assistance from parents so as to help children to uncover *all alternatives,* and to evaluate each and to choose the more enhancing.

        (6) Through role playing (pretending you are the other person in a conflict or dispute, etc.) children are confronted with problems of the kind that will enable mother and father to lead the

family members into a reasoned appraisal of behavior in any given situation. Questions would include, "What would have been right?" "What other things could have been done by those involved?" "Despite the immediate effects, what would or may be the long term effects of this decision or that action?"

(7) In the discussion of personal situations with children, questions should be asked and comments made both about possible problems as well as actual problems.

(a) What would have been the fair thing to do? What actions taken in this situation were "good?" What actions were "bad?" How could they have been improved?

(b) Would you want to have had the same thing done to you?

(c) Was respect shown in this situation? Who acted as gentlemen? Who acted as ladies should? How does such action help solve personal problems?

(d) What would you have done in this situation? Why? Would your actions have enhanced just you? Deprived anyone else? Built understanding and cooperation or destroyed unity and harmony? Contributed to further conflict and misunderstanding?

(e) Children must be taught that in order to gain respect from others they must show respect for others. If they want fairness they must learn to be fair. If they wish justice they must also be just. *They cannot expect* people to keep their promises unless they in turn keep their own word or promises.

(f) Children should be given numerous opportunities to exercise self-discipline.

B. Parents must clearly understand the difference between the democratic ideal which places a high premium upon the establishment of personal standards of rectitude, and the goal of the dictatorship which demands that its people live according to externally prescribed modes of behavior which are enforced through coercion and fear.

1. Parents should strive consistently to create in the home an atmosphere in which it is easy to establish and maintain personal standards of rectitude.

a. Specific acts by a child, which show evidence of personal standards, are recognized by each parent, and the attitude reinforced by direct and positive comment upon the action.

(1) Children must be given favorable consideration for telling the truth about something they have done even though it was against the rules. ("Fear makes some men Great Liars.")

(2) Children are complimented for keeping their promises, particularly when some sacrifice or work was demanded.

(3) Children are recognized for consistently being on time, and accepting and carrying responsibilities for the good of the family.

(4) Outstanding examples of honesty, such as when a child turns in or returns lost money or possessions that he might have kept, are commended before the rest of the family.

(5) Children are offered respect and affection when they voluntarily (even though reluctantly) make changes in their plans in order to help or participate in family matters.

b. Guidance is deliberately *offered* each child to help him develop his own attitudes and standards.

(1) Mother and father should provide many opportunities for children to discuss the "right" and "wrong" in actual situations which may arise during the day — at home, at school, at work, or at play.

(2) Encourage each child to present examples of difficult situations and then to act out desirable solutions with others in the family (or just parents), suggesting alternatives to be considered and tested.

(3) Parents set example of sharing rectitude by their own actions.

(4) Any question seriously proposed by a child concerning standards and conduct is given careful consideration by all members of the family as well as the parents.

2. Parents should refrain as much as possible (consistent with age of children) from using fear to secure actions consistent with externally prescribed "modes of behavior" (family adopted rules and regulations). NOTE: With very young children fear may be an essential factor in protecting the safety, health and welfare of the child and/or family.

   a. Attempt to use reason rather than force in securing adherence to necessary rules for home and family. (NOTE: This does NOT mean that there are no occasions when force will not be a necessary tool to accomplish the end desired; it does mean that it should NOT be the first and only recourse to obtaining compliance.)

      (1) Children should discuss (among themselves and with parents) how family rules help everyone in sharing specific values.

      (2) Children should discuss and help parents define what constitutes unacceptable behavior and what specific steps should be taken if and when it occurs.

      (3) Children should discuss the reasons for these rules, and suggest new ones and changes in old ones when the need for change is obvious.

      (4) Children should discuss how cooperation may be obtained from everyone in observing rules — and how to "educate" stubborn family members so that they will cooperate.

      (5) External control is used only as a last resort to gain adherence to the rules

which are absolutely necessary for the safety, health, and welfare of the individual and family.

b. Parents should strive to refrain from establishing a series of inflexible rules for behavior other than those directly related to safety, health, and welfare of the individual and family. (Note the difference here between "rules for behavior" and the "house rules" in A.1.d.3.)

   (1) Rules which must be set up are made flexible to coordinate with the various levels of maturity and experience of each child in the family. The three-year old can't be as mature in judgement and experience as the fourteen-year old!

   (2) Parents strive to present family rules as guides for maintaining safety, health and pleasant relations, rather than as ironclad rules to be observed because "I say so."

C. Parents and their children should assume personal responsibility for their own behavior.

   1. Parents and their children should each determine and agree on their individual responsibility in carrying out commitments.

      a. Children will find what it means to make and keep promises to parents, friends and others.

      b. Children should be promptly recognized for carrying out family assignments.

      c. Children should discuss what obligations must be fulfilled if one is to be given, or is to earn, special privileges and responsibilities.

    d. Children will have opportunities to determine whether or not (and acceptable ways "how") to try to "get out" of bargains they have made.

2. Parents and children should respect each other's property rights.

    a. Starting from earliest infancy children should be taught and learn when other people's property should not be touched or taken.

    b. Children should each have a special place to keep their belongings; this should be respected by every member of the family.

    c. Children should be taught and practice returning things they have borrowed.

    d. Children must learn to take care of other family members' possessions when they borrow or use them.

    e. Children should find out why flowers should not be picked from other people's gardens.

    f. Children should help care for public buildings – schools, churches, etc.

    g. Children should help protect neighborhood trees, gardens, parks, playgrounds, etc.

    h. Children should learn to report (without fear) and help to repair or replace property they have damaged.

    i. Children should learn the importance of keeping accurate accounts of their own allowance and money entrusted to them (or other property in clubs, scouting, camping, classes, etc.).

    j. Parents should be careful with all property borrowed from their children.

    k. Parents should borrow children's property only with his/her permission.

    l. Parents should set good examples in taking care of family property and possessions.

    m. Parents should respect privacy of children's drawers, etc., except in those few instances where the safety, health or welfare of the child or the family may be concerned.

3. Parents and children should assume responsibility for being truthful, honest and considerate of each other and of others.

    a. Children should learn when it is important to tell what actually happened.

    b. Children should learn to distinguish occasions when truth is required from them; when imagination can be used in the interest of maintaining the well-being of others. (Truth is seldom a defense for rudeness, crudity, or causing pain.)

    c. Children should be given opportunities to learn that by taking the blame for something they have done, they not only increase their status of rectitude and also of respect, but gain in maturity ("growing up").

    d. Children should learn when it is necessary "to report" another child for anti-social behavior (for his or others safety, health or welfare), and when tattling (for personal gain or to get someone in trouble) is not desired.

e. Children should learn how to report facts accurately when asked for needed information, or to help settle an argument, or to solve an important problem or situation.

f. Children should help determine how much credit to give others who have helped them complete tasks they have performed ("sharing" begets "sharing").

g. Children should be taught when to offer and when to withhold comments, and why this is essential.

h. Children should learn to distinguish between real fact and unsupported opinion.

i. Parents should tell the truth to their children, but always tactfully.

j. Parents should frankly admit their mistakes, and discuss how they might be avoided in the future.

k. Parents should give credit to each child when credit is due — promptly and before other family members.

D. Children should be encouraged to learn and to practice the skills of according respect and affection to others — *to share* as much as possible.

1. It is not just a "middle class" mode for people to be kind, considerate or well mannered. Rich and poor alike benefit ("value") from social niceties which mark well brought-up persons from those who are rude, crude, thoughtless and boorish. Children therefore, should learn and practice certain social skills which make for pleasant, "caring" and peaceful living in an enhancing atmosphere for everyone, not just themselves.

a. They should be taught and encouraged to write congratulatory, "Thank You" and "Get Well" notes.

b. They should be taught and encouraged to practice *daily*, correct ways of greeting, introducing, and taking leave of others.

c. They should be taught by parents the appropriate skills to be used on special social occasions, and they should practice these at home regularly.

(1) They should learn how to write invitations and how to answer them affirmatively and negatively. (R.S.V.P.)

(2) They should learn how to ask for and accept, or refuse, a dance or other invitation to participate.

(3) They should learn how to express appreciation to host and hostess when visiting, or going to a party, etc.

(4) They should learn the "please" and "thank you" that expresses sincerity (respect).

(5) They should learn proper table manners and etiquette so they can act properly in school, church, meetings, social gatherings, as well as at home.

(6) Boys should learn their role as "men" in relation to women, and women their role in dealing with "men."

(7) They should learn how to "have their say" in a discussion without depriving another by rude interruptions.

(8) They should learn how to pay attention to a speaker without chattering to their neighbor, reading a paper or book, or distracting others.

(9) Since it frequently is necessary, they should learn how to excuse themselves when it is necessary to leave before a meeting, session, or other occasion is over.

(10) They should learn how to prevent or handle embarrassment of themselves and others.

HELPFUL HINTS FOR DEVELOPING RECTITUDE

1. Does each child have a place all of his own where (or in which) he can put and keep his possessions?

2. What is "responsible freedom" as contrasted with just "freedom?"

3. On the following 5-point scales measure your own Rectitude by circling those points where you *honestly* (and *privately,* of course) feel your behavior falls:

    a. How *honest* am I really? (truth, cheating, stealing, trouble-making, disloyalty, doing what is right, etc.)

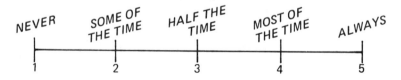

b. How *honest* was I when I answered the previous question?

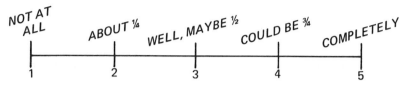

c. How often am I fair?

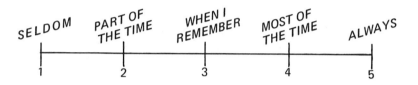

d. Have I ever deliberately broken the law?

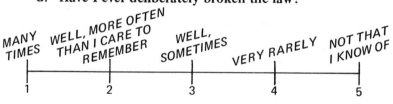

e. How well do I practice what I preach to my children?

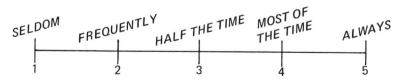

f. Now go back and chart a. to e. on this scale and
    see how you rated yourself. Now rate each of
    your children and compare them with your
    chart.

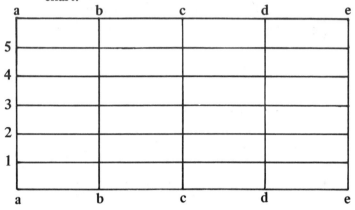

Lastly: burn up all the charts!

4. Give three instances in which parents are justified in
    acting promptly and without prior discussion with
    their children? How should these occasions *later* be
    handled so offspring will comprehend?

5. How can a planned visit to a zoo or farm help you
    teach children the (a) need for parent protection
    (decisions), (b) family relationships, (c) develop-
    ment of individual attitudes and judgement, (d)
    decision-making skills based on growth and matu-
    rity?

6. Describe five (5) ways you can teach your child
    leadership skills and responsibility. (It should start
    by the first birthday, so don't "cop out" by saying
    your children are too young.)

7. What are the *specific* "house rules" for the family? (Tasks, hours, rooms, clothes, baths, going out, letting people in, emergencies, use of telephone, playing with other children at home and at their houses, matches, medicines, parties, cooking, etc., etc.)

8. Do your children understand *each* rule in your answer to No. 7? How long has it been since you went over these with them? (Remember the short retention or memories of many very young children . . . and some not so young!)

9. What family customs or traditions do your children understand and respect because *you* have explained their value and role and practice them? (A *few* examples: grace at meals, "bless you" when people sneeze, family night when no other obligation is allowed to interfere except in true emergencies, dressing for dinner, prayers when going to bed, church or Sunday School, grandmother's for Thanksgiving, monthly family outings, going to concerts and museums, not eating pork, not using any intoxicants, etc., etc.)

10. Have you described how and why other families have different, and seemingly strange, customs and traditions? (Examples: religions and religious practices, clothes and food differences, the Amish and Mennonites and their buttonless clothes and non-use of automobiles, the strong family influence of Japanese and Chinese-American families, use of wines for both food and ceremonial — spiritual — reasons, the meaning of socio-economic as well as racial differences, etc., etc.) Have your children identify as many of these as they have encountered, and then explain the differences and how such differences must be respected, for they are part of what makes a great people (and nation) great!

11. Explain the fundamental difference between "toleration" and "acceptance" of differences.

12. Discuss with *each* child (a) how to be popular and still say "no" (to those invitations that will violate principles); (b) how to be part of a peer group ("gang," club, etc.) and still keep one's individuality; (c) when "conformity" becomes a threat or liability.

13. Ask your children to describe (or write) the kind of person they would really like to be. (You can give them a guide such as (1) height and weight; (2) color and style of hair; (3) body type; (4) personality; (5) clothes; (6) student; (7) athletics; (8) travel; (9) hobbies and skills; (10) talents; (11) kind of friends — age, sex, hobbies, talents, skills, personality; (12) fun and pleasures; (13) tasks, jobs and responsibilities; (14) food; (15) holidays and vacations; (16) church activities; (17) clubs or groups they would like to join; (18) things they like to do best as a family; (19) things they like to do alone with mother; (20) things they like to do alone with father; (21) things they would like to do alone with mother and father; (22) things they like to do solely by themselves.)

If you do this seriously, the resulting pattern or profile can be of inestimable value in helping your child develop sound attitudes, decision-making skills and enhancing behaviors.

14. Name five (5) ways you are giving responsibility (based on age or maturity, of course) to each of your children. Now, below each, add one way you can expand or increase that responsibility as the child becomes able to handle it.

15. With your spouse formulate a realistic set of behavioral goals (or "rules") you would like your children to have. (Note carefully the extent of your differences as well as agreements.)

16. *Without* reference to those formulated by you and your spouse, help your children to formulate a set of possible behavioral rules for themselves.

17. Discuss the differences and similarities (as well as omissions) between No. 15 and No. 16, and arrive at a compromise set which you can all agree to test.

18. Play "I like" with your children. Each person (including mother and father) go around the table and in turn say *one* thing they really like about one person in the family until each person has said something about everyone present.

19. Play "I don't like." Repeat No. 18, only this time each says something about the others that he doesn't like.

20. Play "I would like it better if . . ." Repeat No. 19 only this time each says something about the others that he would like better if they altered or changed something about themselves.

A PARENT'S PRAYER

"Oh, God, make me a better parent. Help me to understand my children, to listen patiently to what they have to say and to understand all their questions kindly. Keep me from interrupting them, talking back to them and contradicting them. Make me as courteous to them as I would have them be to me. Give me the courage to confess my sins against my children and ask them forgiveness, when I know that I have done wrong.

"May I not vainly hurt the feelings of my children. Forbid that I should laugh at their mistakes, or resort to shame and ridicule as punishment. Let me not tempt a child to lie and steal. So guide me hour by hour that I may demonstrate by all I say and do that honesty produces happiness.

"Reduce, I pray, the meanness in me. May I cease to nag; and when I am out of sorts, help me, O Lord, to hold my tongue. Blind me to the little errors of my children and help me to see the good things that they do. Give me a ready word for honest praise.

"Help me to treat my children as those of their own age, but let me not exact of them the judgements and conventions of adults. Allow me not to rob them of the opportunity to wait upon themselves, to think, to choose, and to make their own decisions.

"Forbid that I should ever punish them for my selfish satisfaction. May I grant them all their wishes that are reasonable and have the courage always to withhold a privilege which I know will do them harm.

"Make me so fair and just, so considerate and companionable to my children that they will have genuine esteem for me. Fit me to be loved and imitated by my children. Oh, God, do give me calm and poise and self-control."

Garry C. Myers

Dr. Myers was co-founder and editor of Highlights for Children, a magazine for children, founded in 1946. Dr. Myers died July 19, 1971, and his widow, Caroline Clark Myers, continues to carry on the publication in her late husband's fine tradition.

Underlying Causes of Drug Abuse
. . . And What To Do About Them.

UNDERLYING CAUSES OF DRUG ABUSE

CURIOSITY

PEER GROUP PRESSURE

INSECURITY - DESIRE FOR AFFECTION, IDENTITY
LOW SELF-ESTEEM

BOREDOM - LACK OF EXCITEMENT, ZEST & CHALLENGE IN
CONTRAST WITH STUDY, WORK, ROUTINE

AFFLUENCE & PERMISSIVENESS

ESCAPE - FROM PROBLEMS OF HOME, SCHOOL & SOCIETY

REBELLION AGAINST AUTHORITY

FAILURE

ABSENCE OF STANDARDS & ETHICS - LACK OF MODELS

MENTAL & PHYSICAL PROBLEMS

BUT, wait a moment... look again!

Do you see in these "underlying causes" any that could be "cured" by just TALKING about drugs... just giving students infor- mation (facts) about their effects if abused or misused ?

NO? Then what kind of "causes" are these that young people agree lead them to experiment with dangerous drugs?

If hard-line "Facts" do not change students' minds then the underlying "causes" can only be-

ATTITUDINAL - having to do with emotions, feelings personal reactions

Now, look again... notice how each of the "causes" have to do with PERSONAL FEELINGS and REACTIONS not with facts.

SO... if education is going to effectively prevent drug abuse it is going to have to deal first with —

1. ATTITUDES

2. BEHAVIORS that result when attitudes become decisions to act

3. DECISION-MAKING SKILLS so that every student can learn how to make decisions that will enhance him rather than harm him

EVERY BEHAVIOR HAS ITS CAUSE(S)!

...and every behavior known to man is the result of deprivations or enhancements in one or more of eight "universalities" or "basic needs and wants." These are —

AFFECTION	SKILL
RESPECT	ENLIGHTENMENT
WELL BEING	RECTITUDE
POWER	WEALTH

REMEMBER all human behavior - including drug abuse - is the result of these "needs"

That must mean...

If you cannot satisfy your basic needs in normal ways, you still have the need so...

you must cope with it — you must find an alternative way (behavior) that <u>will</u> supply the need.

If no readily acceptable <u>alternative</u> has been learned — one that satisfies your needs and is also

SOCIALLY ACCEPTABLE

to your fellow men, you <u>will</u> neverthe less find one that does satisfy your needs (because you <u>must</u>) and it will <u>not</u> necessarily be acceptable to others!

AND /

These are "Universalities" – every man, woman & child
regardless of: Race –   Creed –   Origin –
                White   Jewish   Asia
                Black   Catholic   Africa
                Red   Protestant   Europe
                Brown   Mormon   North America
                Yellow   Mohammedan   South America
                etc.   etc.   etc.

and regardless of WHEN he lived – ancient, medieval, or
modern – had or has each and every one of these
universal needs and wants! Some want or need more of
one than another, but each wants & needs some of each
one!

So ... along with the food, clothing and shelter, every man had
to have a satisfying amount of each "universal need"...

WHAT DO THESE CATEGORIES REALLY MEAN?

1. AFFECTION – friendship, love, fondness, loyalty, caring for & being concerned about people.

2. RESPECT – honor, courtesy, recognition, admiration, to be looked up to, to do honor to.

3. WELL BEING – health, happiness, feeling well, contentment.

4. POWER – decision making, influence, authority, leadership.

5. ENLIGHTENMENT – knowledge, education, learning, information, understanding.

6. SKILL – ability, talent, training, capability.

7. WEALTH – food, clothing, shelter, performing a service, property, working, income.

8. RECTITUDE – responsibility, honesty, justice, fair play, trust, keeping one's promises.

LETS GO BACK AND SEE WHAT
AREAS OF DEPRIVATION THE STUDENTS
ARE INDICATING IN THEIR LIST OF
"UNDERLYING CAUSES OF DRUG-ABUSE"

(see if you can pinpoint them!)

UNDERLYING CAUSES OF DRUG ABUSE

CURIOSITY

Anticipated Gains: *Enlightenment, Power, Respect, Well-Being and some Affection.*

Possible Losses: *Rectitude, Well-Being and Respect.*

PEER GROUP PRESSURE

Anticipated Gains: *Power, Respect and even Affection.*
Possible Losses: *Rectitude, Respect, Power.*

INSECURITY - DESIRE FOR AFFECTION, IDENTITY, LOW SELF-ESTEEM

Anticipated Gains: *Affection, Respect, Well-Being, Power.*
Possible Losses: *Rectitude, Respect.*

BOREDOM - LACK OF EXCITEMENT, ZEST & CHALLENGE IN CONTRAST
WITH STUDY, WORK, ROUTINE

Anticipated Gains: *Well-Being, Respect, Power, Wealth.*
Possible Losses: *Rectitude, Well-Being.*

AFFLUENCE & PERMISSIVENESS

Anticipated Gains: *Well-Being, Respect, Power, Wealth.*
Possible Losses: *Well-Being, Rectitude.*

ESCAPE - FROM PROBLEMS OF HOME, SCHOOL & SOCIETY

Anticipated Gains: *Well-Being, Power, Skill, Enlightenment.*
Possible Losses: *Rectitude, Well-Being, Respect.*

REBELLION AGAINST AUTHORITY

Anticipated Gains: *Power, Well-Being, Respect, Enlightenment, Affection.*

Possible Losses: *Rectitude, Wealth, Respect.*

FAILURE

Anticipated Gains: *Affection, Respect, Well-Being, Enlightenment.*
Possible Losses: *Respect, Rectitude.*

ABSENCE OF STANDARDS & ETHICS - LACK OF MODELS

Anticipated Gains: *Power, Affection, Respect, Well-Being.*
Possible Losses: *Respect, Well-Being*

MENTAL & PHYSICAL PROBLEMS

Anticipated Gains: *Well-Being, Respect, Affection, Enlightenment.*
Possible Losses: *Well-Being, Respect, Affection.*

If this is true then it must follow that the same "causes" result in <u>all</u> other behaviors that get young people into trouble when they feel seriously deprived in one or more of the "universal needs and wants"

They cope with their needs by ~

STEALING	DRUNKENNESS
LYING	ASSAULT
VANDALISM	BURGLARY
CHEATING	SEX EXTREMES
CAR THEFT	WAY-OUT LIFESTYLES

... and frequently become delinquents according to society and the law

LET'S-'MBER,
REMEMBER ... That we want attitudes & decisions
HOWEVER ... based on SOUND information & facts, so we
don't overlook this need. Rather, we present
them naturally - as they arise in each class
& relative to the maturity and the "need-
to-know" levels of the students.

The cognitive <u>is</u> important - but must be
presented in a way that doesn't turn
students off! That is why "drug courses" are
NOT advised! The same information should
& can effectually come out in science, history,
geography, civics, government, home economics,
health and language arts courses... and
students WILL learn.

Thus the answer must be to enhance in everyone his own basic "universal needs & wants" so that each learns to cope with his own problems in a manner which is both self-satisfying and socially acceptable.

We must be educated to share the 8 universal values and thereby develop:

    a. Positive attitudes

    b. Decision-making skills

    c. Sense of responsibility

Then and only then will we be able to say to peers & pushers —

WHO NEEDS DRUGS!

NOT I!

BECOMING AWARE OF VALUES by Simpson. Parent/Teacher Resource *Becoming Aware of Values* describes a new teaching method. Specific classroom activities are listed. An excellent section on educational games provides the teacher with ideas to stimulate student participation.

Valuing is based on the premise that each individual has basic needs; for example, affection, responsibility, respect; and that self-esteem depends on the fulfillment of these basic needs. The Valuing process encourages personal growth and development, and helps the teacher encourage self-confidence and a positive self-image in students.

#1/paper/$4.95

BEGINNING VALUES CLARIFICATION by Simon and Clark. Parent/Teacher Resource *Beginning Values Clarification* describes step-by-step how to use values clarification in the classroom. It shows how to help students clarify those things that are important to them. Teachers will find the suggestions and strategies useful, practical and stimulating.

#2/paper/$4.95

GETTING IT TOGETHER by Mattox. Parent/Teacher Resource *Getting It Together* puts Dr. Lawrence Kohlberg's theories on moral development into a readily understood teacher's handbook for use in the classroom. The teacher is provided with detailed information on working with students in the use of the peer group discussion of dilemmas. The large number of dilemmas provided are suitable for use with various age levels, elementary through high school.

#3/paper/$4.95

JUMP TO LEARN by Colwell. Parent/Teacher Resource *The Jump To Learn* program is based on the premise that confidence and self-esteem in young children will grow as they master exercises in coordination and motor skills, such as skipping rope, catching, throwing or running. As the children experience success and gain skills, they also learn to work with other children. It is an indispensible guidebook for anyone working with young children, *Pre-School/Kindergarten*

#4/paper/$6.95

VALUING IN THE FAMILY by Brayer and Cleary. Parent/Teacher Resource *Valuing in the Family* is a workshop guide for parents. It is designed to help parents implement the Valuing process in the home, encouraging respect and self-esteem in family relations. It is written as a guide to help parents understand their children's needs, and to meet these needs through specific methods and activities listed in the book. It is used successfully in a growing number of parent workshops throughout the United States.

#5/paper/$4.95